Beginner's Guide to Drawing and Painting

drawing for the

absolute beginner

A Clear & Easy Guide to
Successful Drawing

Mark and Mary
Willenbrink

NORTH LIGHT BOOKS
CINCINNATI, OHIO
www.artistsnetwork.com

About the Authors

Mark Willenbrink is a freelance illustrator and fine artist whose work has been displayed in fine art shows, with several paintings receiving awards. Mark also teaches art classes and workshops using demonstration, simple instructions and professional tricks to help his students achieve beautiful artwork they can be proud to display.

Mary Willenbrink has her master's degree. She is a Christian counselor and author, but feels her highest calling is to be home to raise her children.

As a husband and wife team, Mark and Mary have authored and illustrated *Watercolor for the Absolute Beginner* (North Light, 2003), and the book has been translated into several languages. Mark's writings and illustrations have been featured in a number of other art instruction books. Mark is a contributing editor for *Watercolor Magic Magazine*. His regularly featured column, "Brush Basics" has been rated as a favorite among the magazine's readers.

Mark and Mary reside in Cincinnati, Ohio, with their three children.

Metric Conversion Chart

To convert	to	multiply by
Inches	Centimeters	2.54
Centimeters	Inches	0.4
Feet	Centimeters	30.5
Centimeters	Feet	0.03
Yards	Meters	0.9
Meters	Yards	1.1
Sq. Inches	Sq. Centimeters	6.45
Sq. Centimeters	Sq. Inches	0.16
Sq. Feet	Sq. Meters	0.09
Sq. Meters	Sq. Feet	10.8
Sq. Yards	Sq. Meters	0.8
Sq. Meters	Sq. Yards	1.2
Pounds	Kilograms	0.45
Kilograms	Pounds	2.2
Ounces	Grams	28.3
Grams	Ounces	0.035

Acknowledgments

We would like to thank those behind the scenes at F+W Publications who have made this all possible: acquisitions editor, Pam Wissman; contracts manager, Julia Groh; editorial director, Jamie Markle; designer, Guy Kelly and production coordinator, Matt Wagner. We would also like to give a special thanks to Pam Wissman for her encouragement to write this book.

To our cherished editor, Kelly Messerly, we would like to give our heartfelt thanks. Your time, patience, talent and encouragement were wonderful! We could not have done this without you!

Thank you, Dorothy Frambes, Mike McGuire and Mary Helen Wallace for sharing your talents so they can be passed on to others.

We would like to thank our mothers, Clare Willenbrink and Grace Patton, who have been such an encouragement to us in our artistic pursuits. Also, thank you to our family and friends for your consistent support.

It is with great pride that we would like to acknowledge our three children for their patience and continuous support while we wrote this book. It is an honor to be your parents. Thank you, thank you, thank you!

It is our encouragement for each other and our unique insights that make this book special. It was fun to write together—which just proves that our marriage, like this book, is a work of art!

Lastly, we thank the Lord for His inspiration. We are all created in our Father's image to be creative, and with our creativity we praise Him.

Dedication

Laus Deo
Praise to God

We would like to dedicate this book to our fathers, Roy Willenbrink and Hugh (Bud) Patton, both of whom we love and miss greatly.

Contents

Chapter 1
Sketching and Drawing

Chapter 2
Principles of Good Drawing

Chapter 3
Value

Chapter 4
Practice the Techniques

Chapter 5
Composition

Chapter 6
Let's Draw

Introduction

Do you remember when you got out your crayons and drew pictures as a child? Now maybe you are proudly displaying your children's artwork on the refrigerator door. You love their pictures because you can see their unique expression in the art, even if it looks more like a Picasso than a Rembrandt. You were just as proud of your own artwork at one time but somewhere along the road of life you began to doubt your artistic abilities. Our belief is that everyone is an artist, and that includes you!

The skills necessary for drawing are not limited just to pencil and paper but can be used in other art forms. When you draw, you are interpreting what you observe from your own perspective. With the principles in this book, you will develop your observational skills, learn the proper tools to use, apply different techniques to your drawing and make use of some of the tricks professionals use every day.

You will learn more if you get out your drawing materials and become an active participant rather than if you just passively read through this book. The material is written to be used again and again. By doing the exercises more than once you will be able to witness the improvement of your artwork.

We hope you will regain that childlike passion for doing art and learning without critiquing yourself harshly. We won't make you hang it on the fridge, but we do suggest you save your artwork because it will show your progress and increase your confidence as you go.

1 Pencils
2 Pencil extender
3 Erasers
4 Angle ruler
5 Pencil box
6 Small sketch pad
7 Large drawing pad
8 Drawing board
9 Pencil sharpener

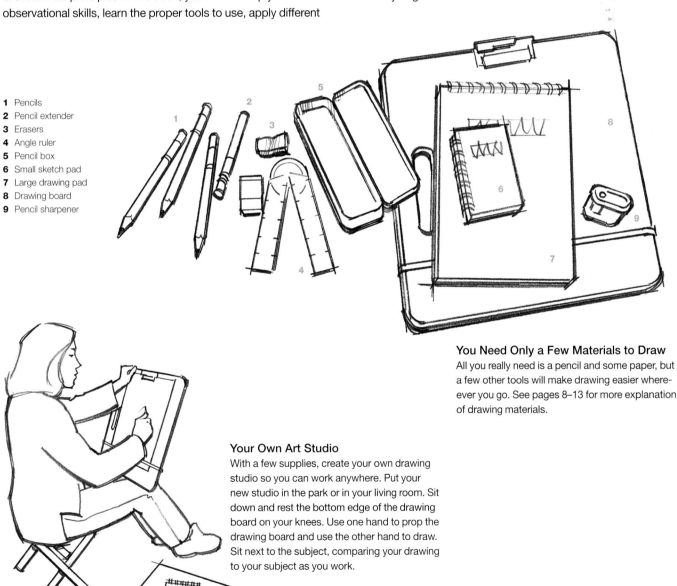

You Need Only a Few Materials to Draw
All you really need is a pencil and some paper, but a few other tools will make drawing easier wherever you go. See pages 8–13 for more explanation of drawing materials.

Your Own Art Studio
With a few supplies, create your own drawing studio so you can work anywhere. Put your new studio in the park or in your living room. Sit down and rest the bottom edge of the drawing board on your knees. Use one hand to prop the drawing board and use the other hand to draw. Sit next to the subject, comparing your drawing to your subject as you work.

Pencils

Though one pencil may look just like any other, there are many different types of pencils to choose from. Each has different uses to achieve a wide range of results. One difference among pencils is the core, which may be made of *graphite*, *carbon* or *charcoal*. I especially like the graphite (commonly mislabeled lead) pencil because it can easily be erased, it comes in many degrees of firmness and it does not easily smear. Carbon and charcoal pencils provide rich, dark colors but they don't erase as well, smear easily and have a very soft feel. Black colored pencils don't smear, but they don't erase well and have a firm but waxy feel.

Pencil Hardness

Hardness is another important quality to consider when selecting pencils. Ratings, usually stamped on the pencils, range from H (hard) to B (soft), with F and HB in the middle. For the demos in this book, we will use 4H, HB and 4B graphite pencils. These will provide a range in hardness without requiring you to keep track of an overwhelming number of pencils. 8B pencils create nice darks, but they are so soft that they need to be continually sharpened.

Keep Your Pencil Choices Simple

4H, HB and 4B graphite pencils are used for the demonstrations in this book, but you may choose to use a different combination of pencil grades or a *mechanical pencil* for your own drawings apart from this book. If you are trying to duplicate the finished drawings in this book, make it easy on yourself and work with the same materials suggested, or you may end up frustrated, wondering why you achieved different results.

Woodless Pencils

Woodless pencils have only a thin coating over their thick cores. This is a novel idea, but woodless pencils are prone to breaking, especially when carried in a pocket! Use pencils with wood surrounding the core instead.

Runaway Pencils!

Use hex-shaped pencils instead of round pencils because round pencils roll and can get away from you.

Pencil Extender

To get more miles out of your pencils, use a pencil extender on the end of a pencil that has been shortened by use.

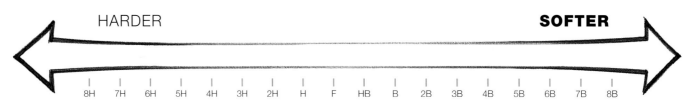

HARDER ← → **SOFTER**

| 8H | 7H | 6H | 5H | 4H | 3H | 2H | H | F | HB | B | 2B | 3B | 4B | 5B | 6B | 7B | 8B |

Pencils Come in a Variety of Hardnesses

Keeping Your Pencil Sharp

If you want to draw a thin line, you will need a sharp point on the tip of your pencil. You can sharpen your pencils in two ways: with a *pencil sharpener* or by hand, using a *craft knife* and a *sandpaper pad*.

Pencil Sharpeners Are the Simplest Way to Keep Pencils Sharp
A pencil sharpener is the quickest and easiest way to keep the tips of your pencils sharp.

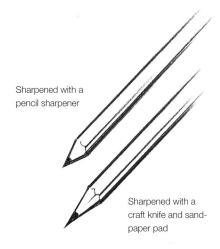

Sharpened with a pencil sharpener

Sharpened with a craft knife and sandpaper pad

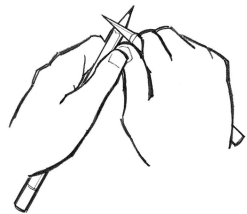

A Craft Knife and Sandpaper Pad Reveal More of the Pencil's Core
For a controlled point that exposes more of the core, sharpen your pencil with a craft knife and sandpaper pad.

First Shape the Pencil With a Craft Knife
Grip the pencil in one hand, with the point away from you, and the craft knife in the other. Push the thumb holding the pencil against the thumb holding the knife to create leverage so the blade cuts into the pencil. Cut, then turn the pencil and repeat the process until you've worked the area into a point.

Identifying Your Pencils
To avoid having to search and squint to read the markings on the sides of your pencils, label the pencil ends with nail polish or colored tape. Place the nail polish or tape toward the top of the pencil, but avoid covering the rating stamp or placing it where the pencil extender would cover it.

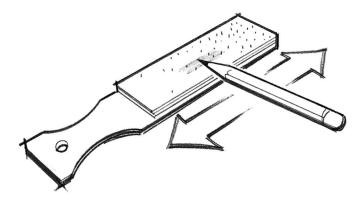

Then Sharpen the Core With a Sandpaper Pad
Sand the core back and forth on the sanding pad for a sharp point.

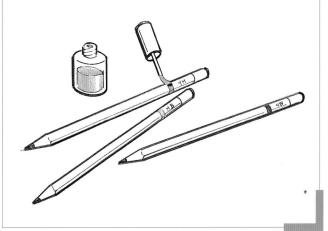

Paper and Drawing Board

Papers for sketching and drawing vary in size, weight, surface texture (usually referred to as *tooth*) and content. They may also be categorized as either sketch or drawing paper. When choosing drawing paper, always choose an *acid-free paper,* or the paper may yellow over time. *Sketch paper*, as the name implies, is for sketching and usually has a *paper weight* of 50 to 70 lbs. (105gsm to 150gsm). *Drawing paper*, which is for more finished art, usually comes in 90-lb. (190gsm) weight. A small 6" × 4" (15cm × 10cm) pocket sketch *pad* is great for quick studies and ideas, while larger sketch pads are obviously needed for bigger sketches. Any drawing you begin may be completed as a keeper, so you may prefer to begin all your drawings using an 11" × 14" (28cm × 36cm) medium-tooth, acid-free, 90-lb. (190gsm) drawing paper.

The lights and darks in a drawing are achieved by varying the amount of pressure applied to the pencil. Because of this, it is necessary to have a hard surface beneath the paper, ideally a *drawing board*. It offers a smooth, solid surface without surprise ruts or nicks, and it won't bend or give with pressure the way the cardboard back of a drawing pad can.

Sketching and Drawing Paper
Use both a small sketch pad and a larger drawing pad. Tear out the individual drawing pad sheets and use them on a drawing board.

Drawing Boards Provide a Hard, Smooth Surface
Drawing boards can be bought with a clip attached to one end and a rubber band on the other to hold a sheet of paper in place.

Tracing Paper and Masking Tape

Use *tracing paper* to make a more refined sketch. Put the previous sketch under the top sheet of tracing paper. Use masking tape to secure the sheets of paper to each other, then carefully trace the desired elements of the image onto the tracing paper.

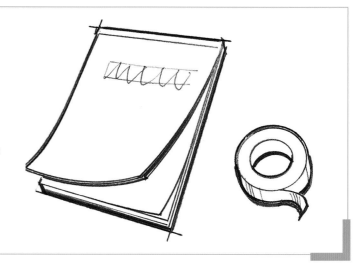

Erasers

Erasers are the sort of thing to have with the idea that you will use them only sparingly. Each time you use an eraser, you risk smearing the drawing or damaging the paper.

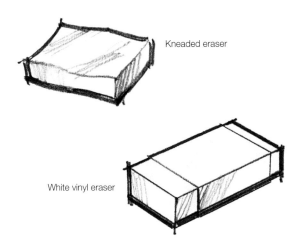

Kneaded eraser

White vinyl eraser

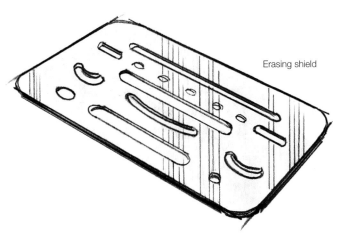

Erasing shield

Kneaded Eraser

The first eraser you get should be a *kneaded eraser*. These soft, putty-like erasers are very gentle to the paper's surface and leave few, if any, crumbs. To erase, first try pressing the eraser to the paper's surface; this is less damaging to the paper than rubbing the eraser back and forth.

White Vinyl Eraser

Use a *white vinyl eraser* to remove hard-to-erase pencil lines. White vinyl erasers are more abrasive than kneaded erasers but will not stain the paper, as some colored erasers often do. White vinyl erasers leave behind strings rather than crumbs, making cleanup easy.

Erasing Shield

Made of thin metal, an *erasing shield* masks the areas that are not to be erased. To use it, with one hand firmly hold the shield down over the area not to be disturbed and, with your other hand, carefully erase over top of the shield.

Avoid Using the Eraser at the End of Your Pencil

Never use the eraser at the end of a pencil. It may smear pencil lines and stain the paper.

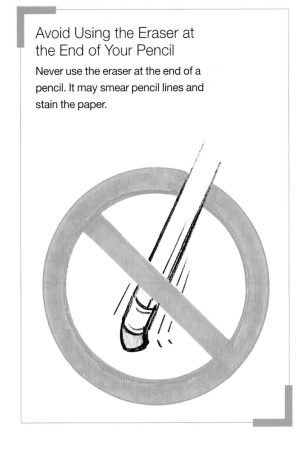

Additional Drawing Tools

In addition to the basic supplies, there are other tools that will help make your drawing experience easier and more enjoyable.

Straightedge

Using a *straightedge* will give you sharp, accurate lines when your subject is technical and requires precision. The precision from a straightedge would look awkward in a sketchy drawing, though. If you want straightedge accuracy without the tightness, use the straightedge during the sketching stage with a light pencil line, then draw over those lines more heavily freehand in the drawing stage.

Triangle

Because it is larger than a ruler and has more surface area to grip, a *triangle* can be easy to use for drawing straight lines.

T-Square

Using a triangle with a *T-square* hooked to the side edge of your board or drawing pad will help you draw more precise vertical, horizontal and diagonal lines. This method is best used for drawing technical subjects such as buildings in linear perspective (see pages 32–38).

Angle Ruler

An *angle ruler* works like a ruler, but it can pivot to measure angles and can fold small enough to fit in a pencil box. See page 30 for instructions on using this tool to draw angles.

Dividers

Dividers are used to observe and duplicate proportions from a photo or sketch. See page 29 for instructions on using standard dividers.

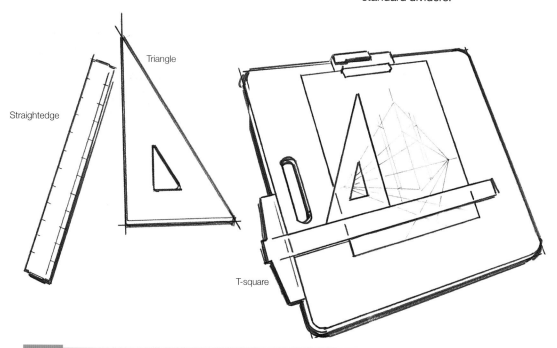

Straightedge

Triangle

T-square

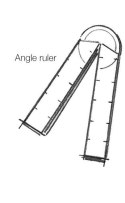

Angle ruler

Must-Have Materials
- 4H, HB and 4B graphite pencils
- Pencil sharpener
- Sketch pad
- 11" × 14" (28cm × 26cm) medium-tooth drawing paper
- Drawing board
- Kneaded eraser
- White vinyl eraser

Optional, But Not to Be Overlooked
- Straightedge, triangle or angle ruler
- Light box

- Dividers, proportional dividers or sewing gauge
- Small mirror
- Erasing shield
- Pencil extender
- Craft knife
- Sandpaper pad
- T-square
- Fixative
- Tracing paper
- Masking tape

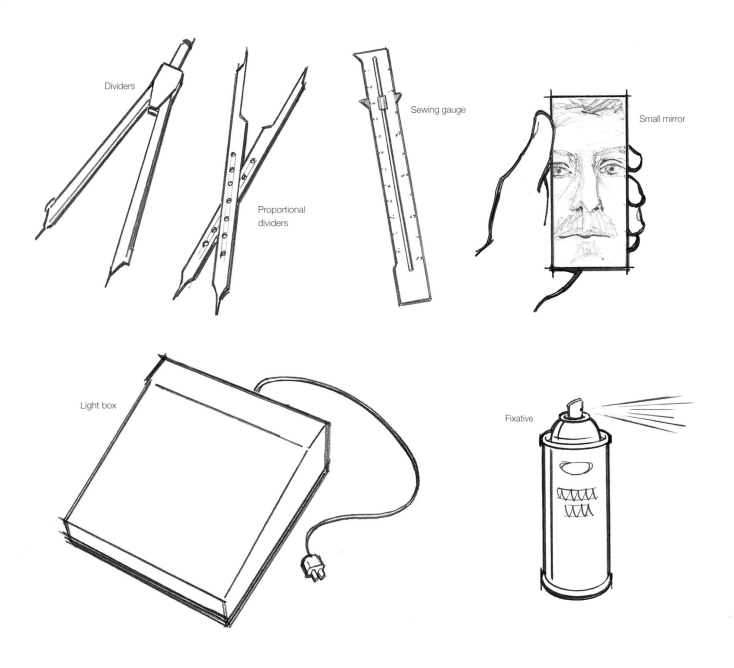

Dividers

Proportional dividers

Sewing gauge

Small mirror

Light box

Fixative

Proportional Dividers
Proportional dividers are used to proportionally enlarge or reduce a image. (See page 29 for additional instruction.)

Sewing Gage
A *sewing gauge* is an inexpensive tool that can be used to measure the proportions of a still life, three-dimensional subject matter, or when working from flat reference materials such as photographs.

Light Box
A *light box* allows you to work from a structural drawing without having to sketch guidelines directly on your drawing paper. This process is explained in more detail on page 24.

Small Mirror
Use a small mirror for self-portraits and for observing facial features. It is also handy for examining your artwork in reverse form. Looking at a drawing in reverse will allow you to see the composition through fresh eyes.

Fixative
Fixative is a spray applied to pencil drawings to prevent the artwork from smudging. It's used mostly for carbon or charcoal drawings, which tend to be powdery. For the demos in this book, fixative isn't necessary because you'll be drawing with graphite. Graphite is not likely to smear if the drawings are stored loosely, one on top of the other.

1 Sketching & **Drawing**

Sketching and *drawing* are two different things. A *sketch* is a work in progress. You may sketch to observe your subject matter or to resolve questions regarding a drawing you are working on. A sketch may help you understand the values of a subject, or gain more understanding of the subject's structure, proportions and placement of its compositional elements. Sketches like these may progress toward a more finished drawing. On the other hand, (no pun intended!) *drawing* is an activity that is begun with the intention of producing a finished piece of art.

With these definitions in mind, recognize that there are times to begin a drawing with a sketch and there are times to begin a sketch without any intention of refining it into a finished drawing. As a beginner, if you are trying to do more drawings than sketches, then you may be putting too much pressure on yourself. Loosen up and enjoy learning four different approaches to sketching and drawing: structural line sketching, value sketching, black-and-white sketching and contour sketching.

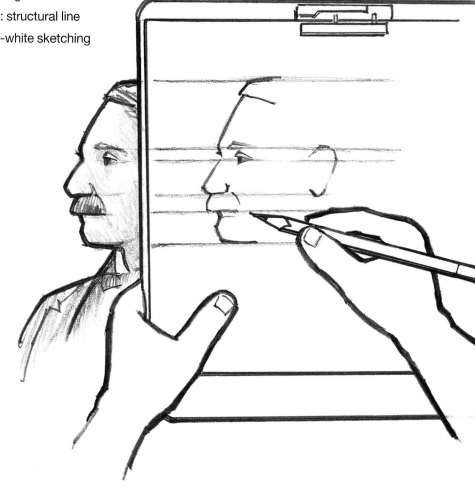

Let the Lines Guide You
Line up your drawing board and paper with your subject and lightly sketch horizontal lines. These will guide you as you place your subject's features. Grab a friend and try it yourself!

Holding the Pencil

There are different ways to hold a pencil, depending on what type of strokes and lines you want to achieve. You may start out with loose, sketchy lines and progress to tighter, more controlled lines and shorter strokes. Here are some common hand grips you can try as you sketch and draw. You may find something else that works better for you. You will find that pressure and grip affects the line results of your drawings. Generally, the more pressure you apply, the darker your line will be.

Create Thick, Loose Lines

For thick, loose lines, avoid using the point of the pencil. Instead, grip the pencil with your thumb and fingertip so that the pencil lead lies flat against the paper. Your fingertips should be either just above the paper surface or gently resting on it. This may smear your previous pencil lines, so be careful. You will use your entire arm to draw these wide lines.

Create Thick, Tight Lines

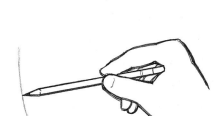

Apply more pressure to the point of the pencil by moving your index finger closer to the tip. Your fingertips may rest on the paper, though it isn't necessary that they do so for this stroke to be successful.

Create Thin, Controlled Lines

For lines like these, grip the pencil as in a handwriting position, with the pencil resting between your thumb, middle and index fingers. Your hand rests gently on the paper. For very thin lines, the pencil tip needs to come to a sharp point.

Create Long, Arcing Lines

This grip is similar to the handwriting position, except you hold the pencil out at length. Use this grip to achieve wide, straight and arced lines. Let your hand rest gently on the paper.

Using a Frisket

A piece of paper can be used as a *frisket* to make an even edge for a set of pencil lines. This is also a great technique to use if you want to create a clean margin for your drawing. This method also works well for backgrounds.

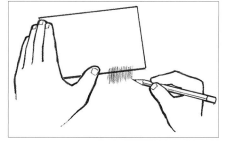

Cover the Drawing

Place a piece of scrap or copier paper over your drawing. Start the line strokes on the scrap paper and continue onto the drawing paper.

Lift the Frisket

Lift your frisket away. The pencil lines should look as if they start from one invisible line.

Structural Sketches

A *structual sketch* is the basic linework in which values and details are built upon. They are a great way to observe your subject, and are often used as a basis for a more finished drawing. A structural sketch is also an excellent way to loosen up before doing another type of sketch or drawing.

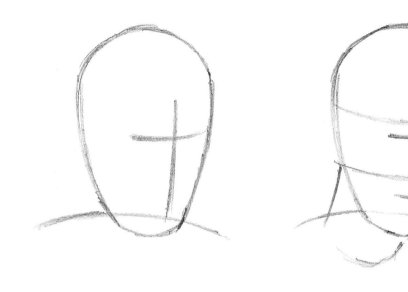 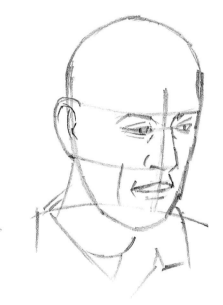

Focus on the Basic Structure
A structural sketch will help you observe and understand the underlying structure of the subject. Here you will focus on the placement and proportions of the elements rather than on light or shadows (see page 18).

Structural Sketch of a Coffee Cup

A structural sketch helps you see how a subject is constructed. Look for basic shapes such as squares, rectangles and circles. Now ask yourself how they relate to one another. Before you pick up your pencil to sketch your coffee cup, take a minute to study your subject.

Must-Have Materials

4H graphite pencil
Drawing paper
Kneaded eraser
Straightedge (optional for the first step, absolutely prohibited for the rest of the steps)

Structural guideline

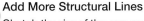

1 **Sketch the Basic Form and Structures**
Use a 4H pencil to sketch the outer forms of the mug and the most relevant structural guidelines, such as those that will indicate the placement of the rim, the bottom of the cup and the handle.

2 **Add More Structural Lines**
Sketch the rim of the cup and the handle. Use the lines you drew in step one to help you add these additonal lines. Look for points where elements line up such as the rim of the cup and handle.

3 **Add Detail Lines to Finish**
Add details such as the inner lines of the rim and handle. Erase any unnecessary guidelines with a kneaded eraser.

Value Sketches

Values are the degrees of lights and darks in a drawing or painting. A *value sketch* is used to observe a subject without much regard for structural or proportional accuracy. Here you focus on the lights and darks of your subject. One way to visually separate the structural lines from the values is to squint at your subject. This blurs the structural lines and makes the lights and darks more noticeable. For a finished drawing that employs values, it's a good idea to do a structural sketch first to make sure the elements of your subject are in the right places. See page 24 for more explanation of combining drawing approaches.

Use Layers of Shading for Value Sketches
Begin a value sketch by first locating the areas of highlights, which will be left white. Then lightly shade the areas of overall values. The next step is to add more layers of shading for the middle values. Finally, add the darkest shading.

Using an Erasing Shield

If you want to erase in a specific area of your drawing, use an erasing shield. Place the erasing shield over the region that is not to be erased. Gently begin erasing with a kneaded eraser. Use a white vinyl eraser if the kneaded eraser doesn't fully erase the first time.

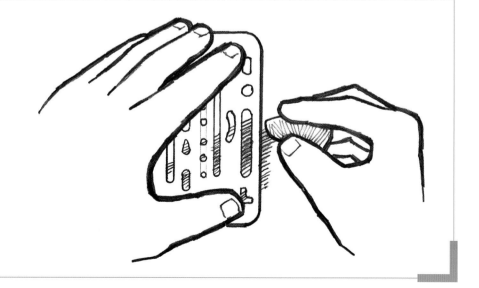

Value Sketch of a Coffee Cup

MINI DEMONSTRATION

In this exercise you will be focusing on values instead of lines. The idea of a value sketch is to define form through light and shadow instead of lines, so use shading to give your coffee cup form. Remember, this is not intended to be a finished drawing, so relax and enjoy the process.

Must-Have Materials
4B graphite pencil
Drawing paper
Kneaded eraser

1 Sketch the Lighter Values
Use a 4B pencil to sketch the lighter values, keeping the lightest ones the white of the paper. Use pencil strokes that feel comfortable for you. They may be vertical, horizontal or even scribbles.

2 Sketch the Middle Values
Continue adding layers for the middle values, gradually giving form to the sketch.

3 Sketch the Dark Values
Finish by adding more layers for the darkest values. Use a kneaded eraser to lighten some areas if you think they need it.

Black-and-White Sketches

Black-and-white sketches are like value sketches, except that you focus on the contrasting blacks and whites and ignore the middle values. Your softest 4B pencil will work, but charcoal and carbon pencils work especially well for this because of their rich, dark qualities. Also called *chiaroscuro* sketching, this type of sketch is a good exercise for understanding what makes images visually identifiable with the most basic of values, black and white.

No Outlines or Middle Values Allowed
No matter what part of the subject you're drawing, use only black and white forms to define it for a *Chiarosuro* drawing.

Avoid Smudges

As you are drawing, your hand glides over the paper surface and can smear the pencil lines. One solution to this is to use a *slip sheet*, which is a sheet of paper placed between your hand and the drawing surface. This way your hand does not rest directly on the drawing.

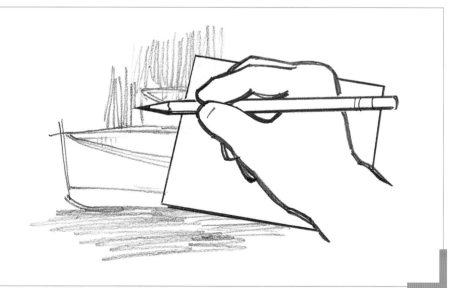

Chiaroscuro Coffee Cup

No, it's not a fancy type of coffee, it's a black-and-white sketch of a coffee cup! This is like taking a value sketch to the extreme; no outlines and no middle values will be used to interpret the subject. Use this method to examine a subject's most basic lights and darks.

Remember, this is just a study. Like a sketch, this is not intended to look like a finished drawing.

Must-Have Materials
Anything from a 4B to 8B graphite, carbon or charcoal pencil
Drawing paper
Kneaded eraser

1 Start With the Most Obvious Darks
With a soft-lead pencil, sketch the most noticeable darks of the subject. In this case, the interior of the mug, along the rim, and down the right on the outside of the mug are the darkest areas. Keep your pencil strokes close together so areas will look black.

2 Add More Darks
Continue adding darks, using them to define the image.

3 Add a Background
Finish adding darks to complete the mug. Add a background and some shadows to further define the image.

Contour Sketches

This type of sketch is also called a *continuous line sketch* because you draw with one continuous line, drawing outlines and defining value areas. Don't worry about accuracy. This is a fun exercise for loosening up before you draw, and it will sharpen your observation skills. Add more of a challenge by blocking your view of the sketch in progress, letting your hand guess at what the pencil line looks like on the paper. This is called *blind contour sketching*.

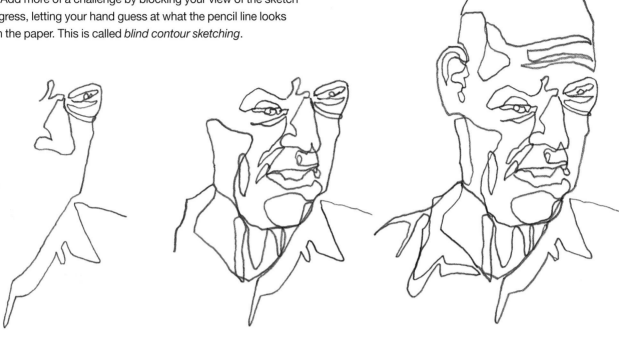

Continuous Line Sketch
Once you start moving your pencil, don't lift it until the sketch is done.

Blind Contour Sketch
This sketch was done by observing the subject without looking at the drawing paper. Block your view of the sketch with a piece of cardboard until you're finished.

Blind Contour Sketches Help You Understand Your Subject
No one expects contour sketches to be identifiable. As Mary worked through this sketch, she gained a real understanding of the contours of her coffee cup.

Contour Sketch of a Coffee Cup

MINI DEMONSTRATION

This sketch is done by placing the pencil onto the paper and not lifting it until the sketch is finished. Look for lines and shapes. Follow the contours that define the subject and the shadows around it. Doing a contour sketch is truly an exercise in putting observation into practice!

Must-Have Materials

HB graphite pencil
Drawing paper
Kneaded eraser

1 Start Moving the Pencil

Put an HB pencil to the paper and start moving it, following the contours of the subject without lifting the pencil from the paper.

2 Continue the Pencil Movement

Keep moving the pencil so that the sketch is formed with a single line.

3 Finish Up

Keep moving the pencil until the sketch is complete.

Combining Approaches

We've explored four different approaches to sketching and drawing. If you tried the value, black-and-white or contour sketch demos, you might be thinking your art didn't turn out anything like you expected. Do not be discouraged and don't give up! You are already growing in your observation skills.

You can combine some of the different approaches to achieve a more finished drawing. For instance, start with a structural line sketch and then add values. During the structural sketch stage, you should look for the basic shapes (see page 27) and proportions (see pages 28–29) so you can be confident of their placement before you add the values.

A light box is a device that allows you to see the structural lines for a drawing without having to draw them on the artwork itself. First, create a structural sketch of your subject. Place the structural sketch on the light box, then tape a piece of drawing paper to the structural line sketch. The image will be visible through the drawing paper to provide a foundation for your value, black-and-white and contour drawings.

Combine Approaches for a Finished Drawing
Work out proportions with a structural sketch and placement of the elements in your composition. Add value changes to define form and shadow.

A Light Box Makes Combining Drawing Approaches Easy
Do a structural sketch of your subject, erase obsolete guide lines and add detail lines defining the form and shadows. Use this sketch as the basis for a value sketch, black-and-white sketch or contour sketch. Place the sketch on a light box and then place your drawing paper on top of the sketch. Turn on the light box so the image of the sketch will be visible through the drawing paper. This will provide a framework for your subject so you don't have to sketch the structural guidelines onto the drawing paper.

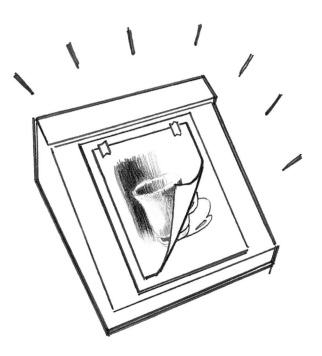

Structural Line Sketch
These lines indicate highlights and shadows as well as the structure of the subject. To use other drawing approaches, erase any obsolete markings.

Value Drawing Using the Structural Line Sketch and Light Box
A light box was used to backlight the structural sketch as a guide for this value drawing.

Black-and-White Drawing (Chiaroscuro) Using the Structural Sketch and Light Box
A light box was used to backlight the structural sketch as a guide for this black-and-white drawing.

Contour Drawing Using the Structural Sketch and Light Box
A light box was used to backlight the structural sketch as a guide for this contour drawing.

2 Principles of **Good Drawing**

Good drawing does not come just from having a skilled or trained hand, but also from your ability to observe your subject matter. In fact, one of the things we love most about art is being able to see how each artist interprets a subject. What is it that gives someone the ability to draw well? It is a matter of learning basic principles, applying them consistently and training the eye to observe the subject. *Observing* invovles noticing the basic shapes, proportions and values of objects rather than thinking of them as "buildings," "trees" or "people." Once you have an understanding of the principles and have trained yourself to observe, it is then only a matter of telling your hand to draw what your eye sees, not what your mind thinks the subject should look like.

Using Basic Shapes

Before you pick up a pencil to begin drawing, take time to observe your subject matter. Look for the basic shapes, then sketch them lightly on your drawing paper, working out the correct proportions of those shapes and determining where each should be in relation to one another. If you have questions about the composition, do a few quick *thumbnail sketches* at this point. Once you decide where to place the major elements of your composition, take your sketch to the next step, adding structural details. Finally, add the values. This method of drawing will help ensure that the results will be proportionally correct.

Must-Have Materials

HB graphite pencil
Drawing paper
Kneaded eraser

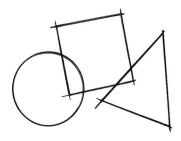

1 Look for the Basic Shapes
Look for circles, squares, triangles, ovals and rectangles in your subject before you sketch.

2 Sketch the Basic Structure
Start with the basic shapes and use them to work out proportions (see page 28) and composition (see page 86).

3 Add Details to the Structural Sketch
Add the details including the columns and trim to the building, define the shape of the trees and add a row of shrubs in front of the building.

4 Add the Values
Add values over the lines to give the scene depth and definition, and to make it look more realistic.

Gauging Proportions

Gauging proportions is as simple as making sure that the *width* and *height* of the objects in your drawing are proportionally similar to those in your reference. Believable art starts with correct proportions, so learning how to gauge proportions accurately will be invaluable. You don't need to know the actual inches or centimeters; instead, measure the *relative* sizes of the elements to achieve an accurate representation of your subject.

There are many tools available for gauging proportions, from a simple pencil to tools made specifically for measuring, such as sewing gauges or dividers. Dividers, both standard and

Gauging Proportions With a Pencil

Gauging Proportions can be done by "measuring" each part of the subject with a pencil. Use the top of your thumb to make the distance from the end of the pencil. Now compare this measurement with those of other parts of the image. In this example, the teapot's height is equal to its width.

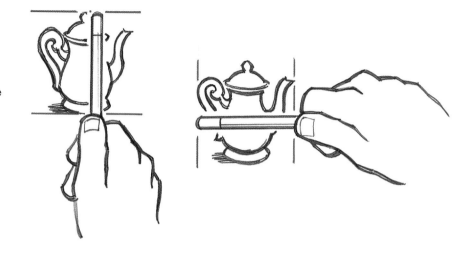

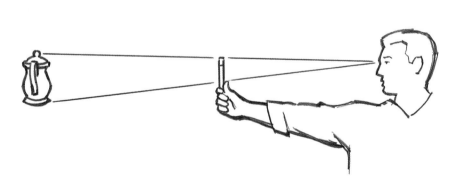

Lock in Accurate Proportions

To correctly gauge proportions in this manner, lock your arm straight in front of you, holding the pencil straight up. Look at the pencil and the subject you're measuring through one eye. A bent arm may result in inaccurate measurements because you may bend your arm at different angles from one measurement to another.

proportional, are used to gauge proportions of two-dimensional reference materials, such as photographs, rather than of three-dimensional objects, such as those in a still-life setup. Proportional dividers enable you to enlarge or reduce by measuring the reference with one end of the tool and then using the other end to determine the size of the image in your drawing.

Proportioning can be done loosely for a quick sketch or more precisely for a finished drawing. The subject also influences how accurate the drawing needs to be. You may be less concerned about the proportions of a tree than you are about the proportions of an automobile.

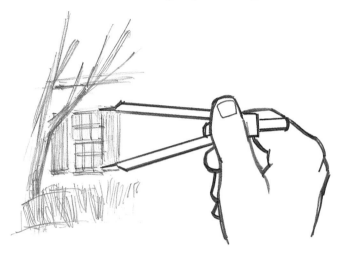

Using Standard Dividers
Measure the subject in your reference with the dividers and transfer the length to your surface. You can only measure a one-to-one ratio with standard dividers. If you wanted to enlarge this window to twice its size, you would have to double the divider's measurement.

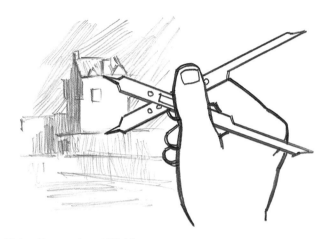

Using Proportional Dividers
Proportional dividers are used not only to compare proportions but also to enlarge or reduce. Measure the subject in your reference with one end of the dividers, then use the other end to mark the measurement for your drawing. The notches in the center of the dividers let you determine just how much you want to enlarge or reduce the size of the image.

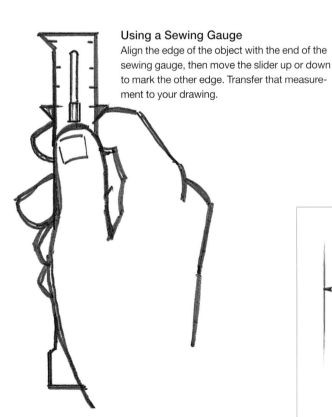

Using a Sewing Gauge
Align the edge of the object with the end of the sewing gauge, then move the slider up or down to mark the other edge. Transfer that measurement to your drawing.

Get It Straight
Straight lines can be drawn using a straightedge or ruler. Another method is to place the side of the hand holding your pencil against the edge of your drawing surface, then glide your hand along the edge.

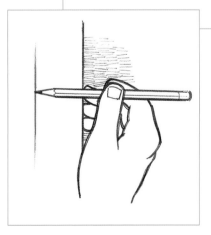

Measuring Angles

Measuring angles sounds technical, but drawing angles mostly involves observation. If you want to take the guesswork out of drawing angles, use an angle ruler. Correct angles will make your drawings more successful.

Duplicate the Angle
First, duplicate the angle of the subject by aligning a pencil with it.

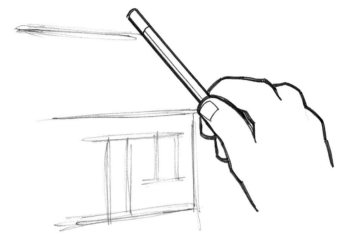

Transfer the Angle to Your Drawing
Keeping the pencil at the same angle, hold it over the drawing and adjust the sketch as needed.

Using an Angle Ruler
An angle ruler (see page 12) also can be used for duplicating angles. Line up the angle ruler with the subject, then hold it over the drawing. Then transfer the angle to the drawing by placing the angle ruler on the relevant area of the drawing and marking along it.

Working From Reference Materials

Images from books, magazines, greeting cards or the Internet that allow you to observe a particular subject are called *reference materials*. It is good to practice observing actual subjects such as the birds in your backyard. Firsthand observation will help you to capture the essence and nature of your subject. The problem with observing from life is that the subject, especially an animal, may not stay still for you. Moreover, the lighting and colors will constantly change. A still life, in which you set up your subject matter with a consistent light source, is another option. You can sit down and take your time observing your subject at your leisure—be sure to warn your family that the fruit bowl is being used for study, or your reference may be eaten by mistake!

Reference Materials
Observation of a subject can be enhanced with reference material. Start a reference file by categorizing photos and magazine pictures in an accordion folder.

How to Approach a Challenging Drawing

Some subjects may seem so daunting, you may not know where to begin. Even finding the basic shapes, which is the best place to begin, may be hard. The following method may help.

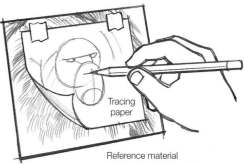

Tracing paper

Reference material

Trace the Basic Shapes
Lay a piece of tracing paper over your reference and trace the basic shapes of the image.

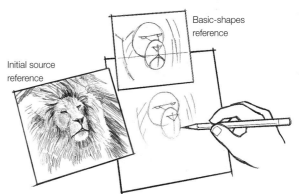

Basic-shapes reference

Initial source reference

Use Your Tracing as a Reference
Use the tracing as another reference to determine the placement of the shapes and their proportions as you begin the drawing.

Understanding Linear Perspective

Perspective is what gives the illusion of depth to a picture. It affects almost everything we see, if only in subtle ways, which is why it is important to have an understanding of how perspective works. Artists employ two types of perspective: *linear* and *atmospheric* (also called *aerial*). Linear perspective involves the use of converging lines and the manipulation of the size and placement of elements within a composition to create the illusion of depth and distance. Atmospheric perspective, which will be explained in more detail on page 41, relies not on lines but on variations in value and detail to achieve similar effects.

Horizon Line

The first step in using linear perspective is to establish a *horizon line* where the land or water meets the sky. The placement of the horizon influences the viewer's perception of a scene and determines where its sight lines should converge. Even when the horizon line is not actually visible, its location must be clear or the perspective of the scene may not be correct (see page 39).

Vanishing Points

Vanishing points occur where parallel lines appear to converge, usually on the horizon. For example, when you look down a train track, the rails seem to converge in the distance. The place where the rails appear to meet is the vanishing point. A single drawing may contain several vanishing points—or none at all—depending on the location of elements within a scene and the *vantage point* of the viewer.

Vantage Point

The best way to describe the vantage point is to say that it is the point from which the viewer observes a scene. In a drawing, the relationship between the location of subject elements (such as trees and buildings) and the horizon line will determine the *eye level* of the vantage point. In addition, the vantage point can influence the mood of a scene (see page 33).

Vanishing point

Vanishing Points
A vanishing point occurs where parallel lines appear to meet in the distance. For instance, when you look down train tracks, the parallel lines of the rails seem to converge at a point on the horizon.

Dog's Eye Level
Placing the horizon low makes the vantage point seem low. In this example, the vantage point is at the dog's eye level. Notice that the horizon line goes through the eye of the dog.

Man's Eye Level
Placing the horizon at the same level as the eyes of the man in the scene puts the vantage point also at the man's eye level. In this example, the horizon line runs through the man's eyes.

Overhead View
With the horizon placed well above the man and dog, the vantage point is also very high. This creates the feeling that the viewer is looking down on both of them.

Low Horizon, Low Vantage Point
With the horizon placed low, the subject may look taller and more massive than normal.

High Horizon, High Vantage Point
A high horizon can give an unnatural feel to a subject that is normally viewed from eye level. Instead, bring the horizon line down to a more natural vantage point.

Vantage Point Can Influence Mood
The placement of the horizon can influence the mood of a scene by creating a variety of sensations in the viewer. Placing the horizon unnaturally low will make the viewer feel as if he were looking up at the subject from a very low vantage point. Placing the horizon unnaturally high will make the viewer feel as if he were looking down on the subject from a great height.

One-Point Perspective

One-point perspective is a simple form of linear perspective with only one vanishing point. Remember to always draw the horizon line first, then determine the placement of the vanishing point on the horizon, which should not be far from the center of the scene. First draw the horizon line, then determine the placement of your two vanishing points on either side of the paper on the horizon line. As you work out the perspective of the elements in the scene, extend the parallel lines either up or down toward the vanishing point, depending on the vantange point you want to create for the viewer.

Let's Get Technical
Use a T-square or triangle with your drawing board. These tools will make technical and perspective drawings easier to do and more accurate.

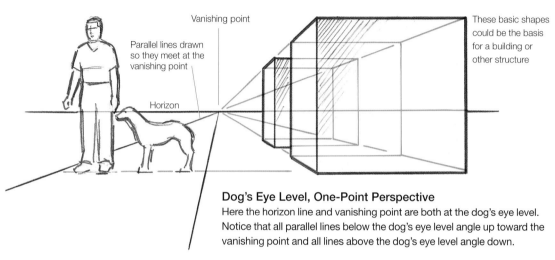

Vanishing point

Parallel lines drawn so they meet at the vanishing point

Horizon

These basic shapes could be the basis for a building or other structure

Dog's Eye Level, One-Point Perspective
Here the horizon line and vanishing point are both at the dog's eye level. Notice that all parallel lines below the dog's eye level angle up toward the vanishing point and all lines above the dog's eye level angle down.

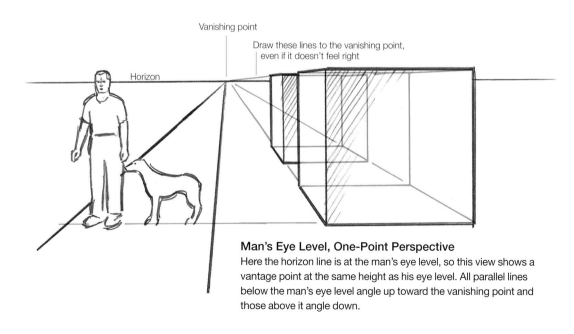

Vanishing point

Draw these lines to the vanishing point, even if it doesn't feel right

Horizon

Man's Eye Level, One-Point Perspective
Here the horizon line is at the man's eye level, so this view shows a vantage point at the same height as his eye level. All parallel lines below the man's eye level angle up toward the vanishing point and those above it angle down.

Vanishing point

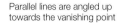
Horizon

Parallel lines are angled up
towards the vanishing point

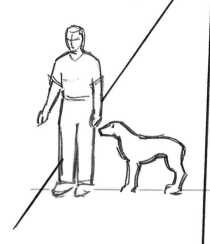

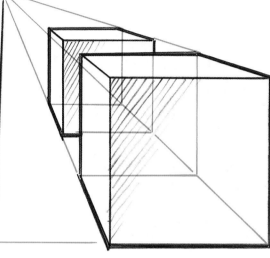

Overhead View, One-Point Perspective

In this view, the horizon is above both the man and the dog. The vantage point is somewhere above the man and the dog creating the feeling that the viewer is looking down on the scene. All parallel lines angle up to converge at the vanishing point.

Principles of Perspective

There are three important principles to keep in mind when you render linear perspective:

- *Depth is expressed by size*. Similar objects will appear bigger if they are positioned closer to the viewer than if they are placed farther away.
- *Depth is expressed by obscurity*. Objects closer to the viewer may hide from view, cover up or cancel out objects that are farther in the distance.
- *Depth is expressed by convergence*. Elements that are parallel to each other will appear to converge in the distance. The point of convergence is called the vanishing point. A scene with linear perspective may have an unlimited number of vanishing points, or none at all.

Two-Point Perspective

Two-point perspective employs the same principles as one-point perspective but with an additional vanishing point. Two-point perspective can give a scene more depth than one-point per-spective. The first object you draw will help you determine the relative sizes of any other objects in the composition.

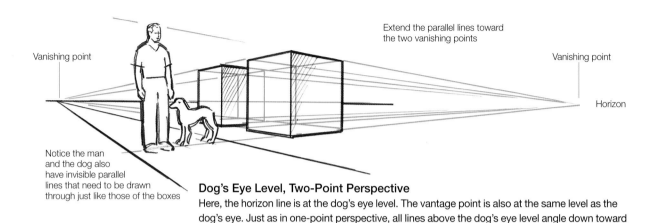

Vanishing point

Extend the parallel lines toward the two vanishing points

Vanishing point

Horizon

Notice the man and the dog also have invisible parallel lines that need to be drawn through just like those of the boxes

Dog's Eye Level, Two-Point Perspective
Here, the horizon line is at the dog's eye level. The vantage point is also at the same level as the dog's eye. Just as in one-point perspective, all lines above the dog's eye level angle down toward the vanishing points and all lines below the dog's eye level angle up toward the vanishing points.

Vanishing point

Extend the parallel lines toward the two vanishing points

Vanishing point

Horizon

Man's Eye Level, Two-Point Perspective
Here, the horizon line is at the man's eye level; the vantage point is at the same level. All parallel lines above him angle down toward the vanishing points and all parallel lines below him angle up toward the vanishing points.

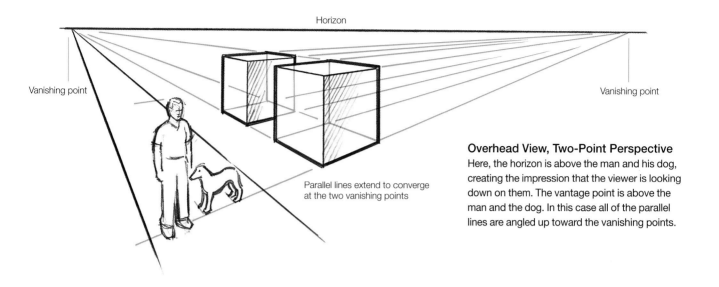

Horizon

Vanishing point

Vanishing point

Parallel lines extend to converge
at the two vanishing points

Overhead View, Two-Point Perspective

Here, the horizon is above the man and his dog, creating the impression that the viewer is looking down on them. The vantage point is above the man and the dog. In this case all of the parallel lines are angled up toward the vanishing points.

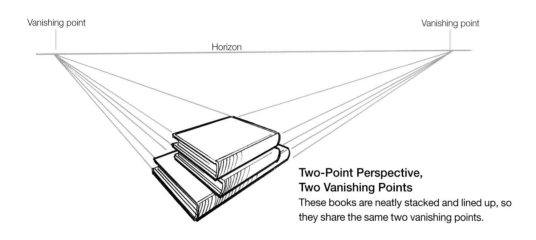

Vanishing point

Vanishing point

Horizon

Two-Point Perspective, Two Vanishing Points

These books are neatly stacked and lined up, so they share the same two vanishing points.

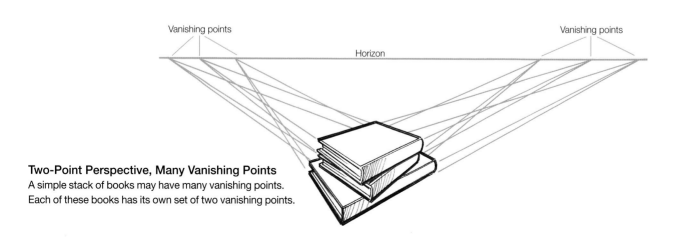

Vanishing points

Vanishing points

Horizon

Two-Point Perspective, Many Vanishing Points

A simple stack of books may have many vanishing points. Each of these books has its own set of two vanishing points.

Three-Point Perspective

Linear perspective may include many vanishing points, as shown by the staggered books on page 37. When you add more vanishing points to a scene, you also add drama and complexity to your composition. If you take a vanishing point and move it high above or far below the horizon, you will create *three-point perspective*.

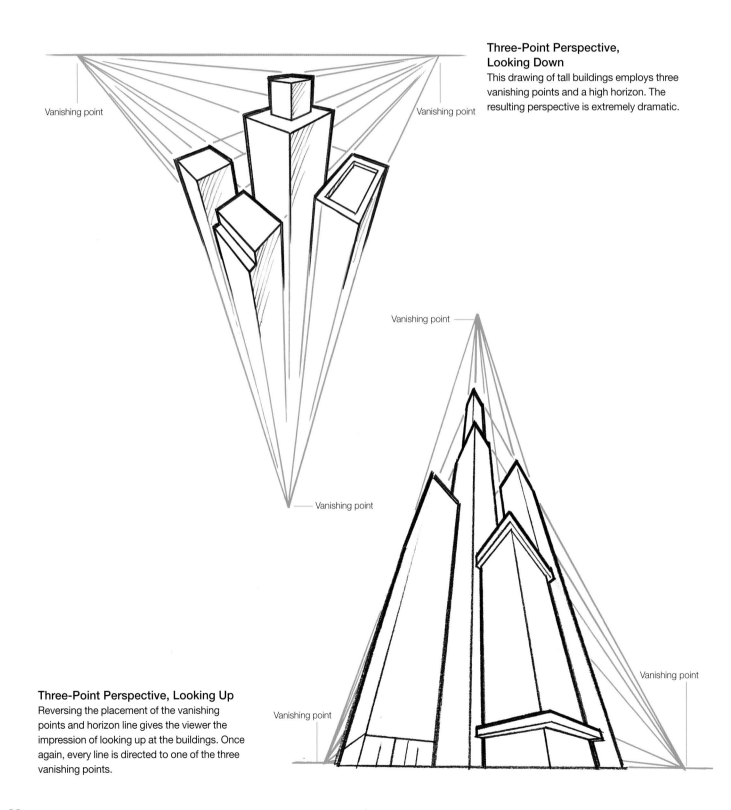

Three-Point Perspective, Looking Down

This drawing of tall buildings employs three vanishing points and a high horizon. The resulting perspective is extremely dramatic.

Vanishing point

Vanishing point

Vanishing point

Vanishing point

Vanishing point

Vanishing point

Three-Point Perspective, Looking Up

Reversing the placement of the vanishing points and horizon line gives the viewer the impression of looking up at the buildings. Once again, every line is directed to one of the three vanishing points.

Hidden Horizons and Vanishing Points

Applying the principles of perspective to all objects in a scene is important, even though horizons and vanishing points aren't always noticeable. They may be hidden behind other elements in the composition, but understanding where they are will help to keep your perspective accurate. If necessary, sketch the horizon and vanishing points lightly with a pencil to make sure perspective is applied to eveything in your drawing. Once you've established perspective, erase your guidelines and finish the drawing.

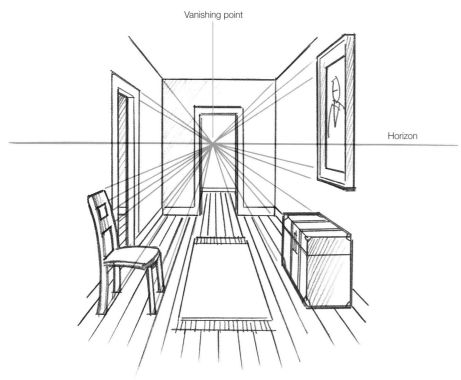

Vanishing point

Horizon

Hide and Seek
Even when the horizon or vanishing points in a scene are hidden, they still affect your drawing. You can easily find your horizon line and vanishing points. If you draw lines from all the parallel elements in this room, they will converge at the vanishing point. Now that you have discovered the vanishing point, you know the horizon line goes through that point in the scene.

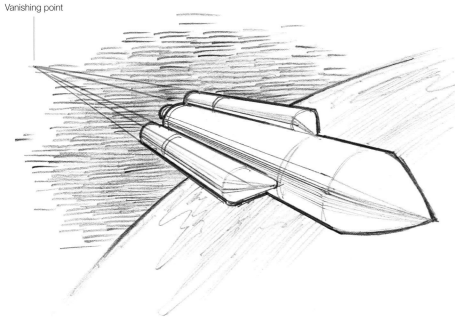

Vanishing point

Beyond the Horizon
Though the subject is not bound to a horizon, this scene still uses the principles of linear perspective.

Locating Vanishing Points

The location of your vanishing points has an important effect on the vantage point of your drawing. The closer the vanishing points are to each other, the closer the object will appear to the viewer. The farther apart they are, the more distant the object will appear to the viewer.

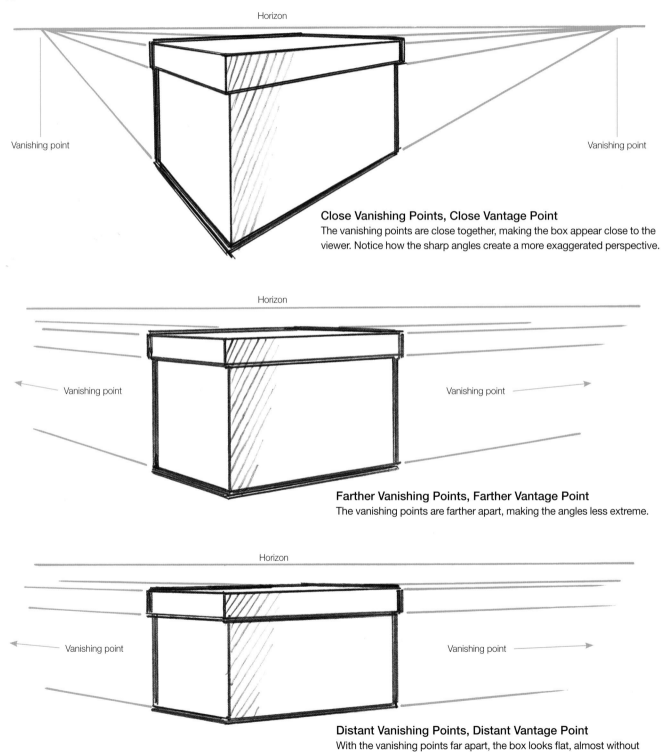

Close Vanishing Points, Close Vantage Point
The vanishing points are close together, making the box appear close to the viewer. Notice how the sharp angles create a more exaggerated perspective.

Farther Vanishing Points, Farther Vantage Point
The vanishing points are farther apart, making the angles less extreme.

Distant Vanishing Points, Distant Vantage Point
With the vanishing points far apart, the box looks flat, almost without perspective. This will give the viewer the impression that the box is in the distance.

Atmospheric Perspective

Atmospheric perspective, also referred to as aerial perspective, uses definition and values to create the illusion of depth and distance. Atmospheric perspective relies on the idea that the closer something is to the viewer, the more it is defined and the more its values contrast. For instance, trees close to the viewer will show more detail and more color variation than trees farther away.

Using Values to Create Depth
In this grouping of trees, the value of the closest trees contrasts more against the background than those farther away.

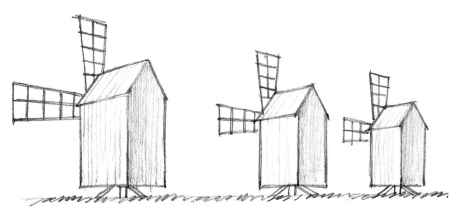

Linear Perspective Only
Depth in this scene relies on the size differences established by linear perspective. The larger windmill seems closer to the viewer than the smaller ones. Atmospheric perspective is not used to show the distance between the windmills.

Atmospheric Perspective Only
All three windmills are the same size, so no linear perspective is used. The only difference is the intensity of their values, which makes them look like they are progressively more distant, going from left to right.

Combined Perspectives
By combining linear and atmospheric perspectives, the depth of the scene is expressed through size and value contrast.

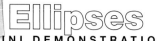

Ellipses

MINI DEMONSTRATION

A circle drawn in perspective becomes an *ellipse* because it follows the same principles as other shapes drawn in linear perspective. An ellipse can be made by first sketching a square in perspective. The lines of the square will be used as the boundaries for the ellipse, because both a circle and a square are equally as wide as they are tall.

Must-Have Materials

4H graphite pencil
Drawing board
Drawing paper
Kneaded eraser
White vinyl eraser

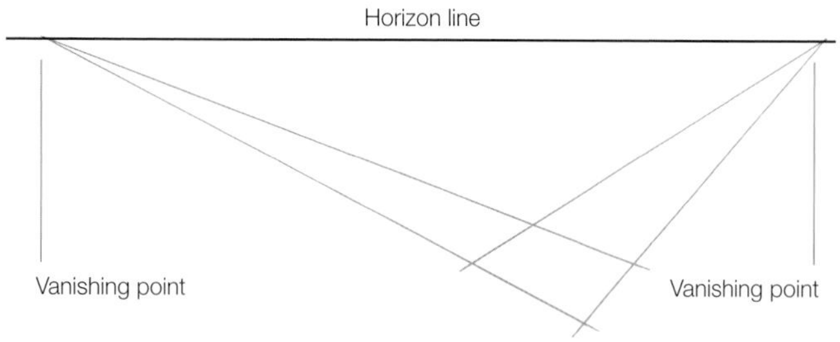

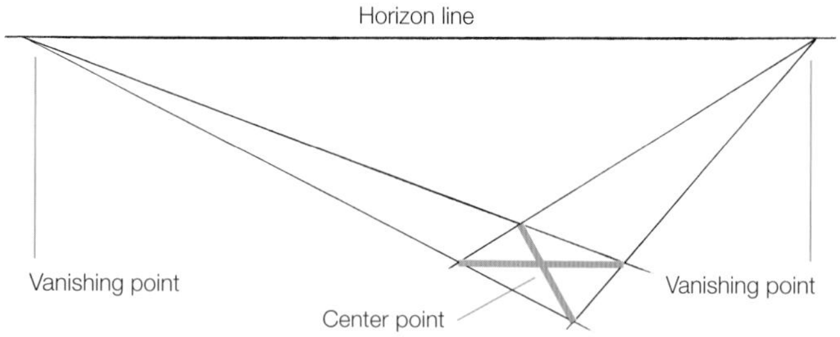

1 Sketch a Square in Perspective
Sketch the horizon line, then place the vanishing points on the horizon. Now sketch a square in perspective by using those vanishing points.

2 Connect the Opposite Corners
Sketch lines connecting the opposite ends of the square. Each line will define the widest and narrowest parts of the ellipse. The intersection of these two lines is the center point of the ellipse.

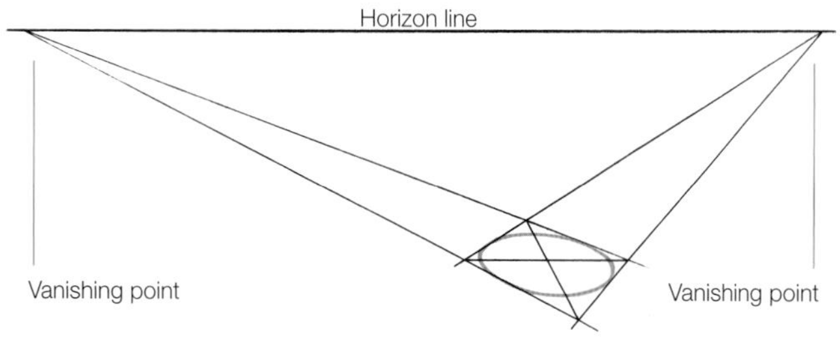

3 Sketch In the Ellipse
Sketch in the shape of the ellipse. Notice that the ellipse is longest in relation to the longest center line.

Ellipses Don't Have Points

Ellipses do not have points on the end. Their ends are round, even if the ellipse is rather flat.

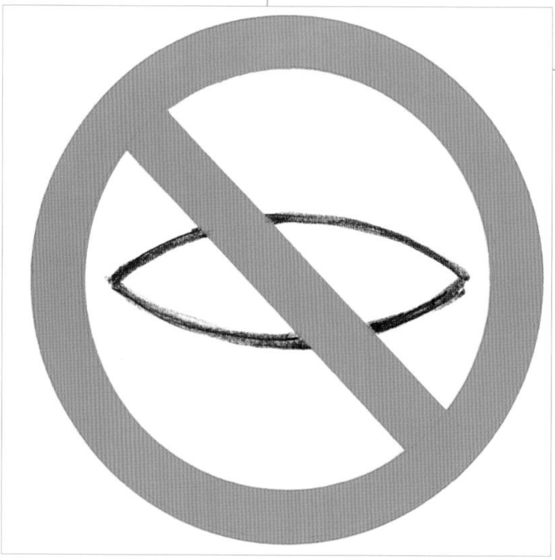

Ellipses In Use

Ellipses can be drawn as vertical, horizontal and angled, but still use the same perspective principles. Remember the first step in drawing an ellipse is to sketch a square in linear perspective.

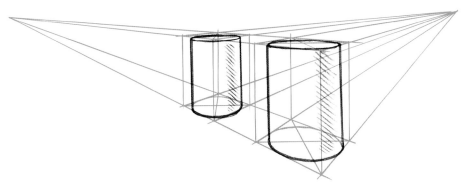

Sketch Cylinders Using Ellipses
The ends of cylinders drawn in perspective are ellipses. First establish the horizon and vanishing points, then sketch the boxes. The ends of the boxes will be the boundaries for the ellipses. Connect the ellipses to create the cylinders.

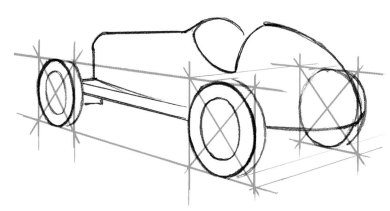

Ellipses Are All Around Us
Ellipses that stand vertically can be drawn in a similar manner. Notice how the center lines direct the shape of each ellipse.

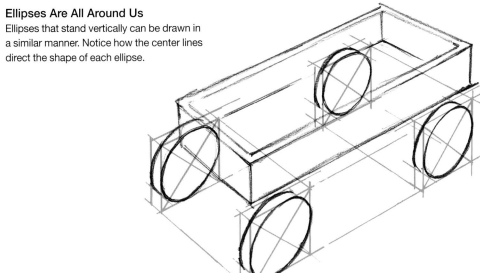

MINI DEMONSTRATION

Circles are not the only curved objects you must draw in perspective. Arches are also quite common and need to follow the rules of perspective to look accurate. The peak of an arch is centered over the space between its supporting walls. The same is true of most roofs. To draw a roof in proper perspective, you will need to know how to find its the center point. Measuring with a ruler will not give you the correct center point as far as perspective is concerned, which is why knowing how to find the center point is important. Try this little exercise to learn how to find the center point for a roof.

Must-Have Materials

4H graphite pencil
Drawing board
Drawing paper
Kneaded eraser
White vinyl eraser

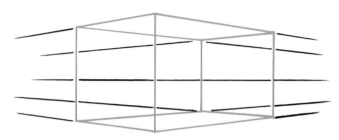

1 Sketch a Rectangle In Perspective
Establish the horizon line, then the vanishing points (which are far off to the left and right). Sketch a rectangle in perspective. This will become the walls that support the roof.

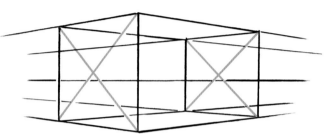

2 Connect Opposite Corners of the Rectangle
Sketch lines connecting the opposite corners of the sides of the rectangle, making two Xs. The intersection of these lines are the center points for the sides.

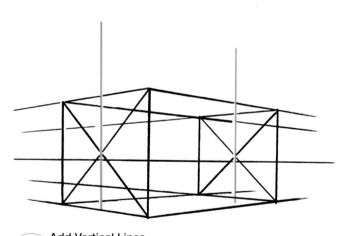

3 Add Vertical Lines
Sketch vertical lines up through the center of the Xs. These lines designate the center of the box's side walls.

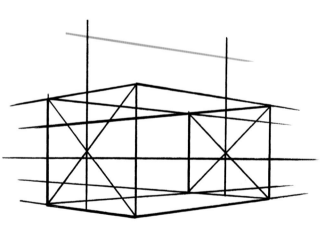

4 Sketch the Top of the Roof
Sketch a line for the top of the roof. If completely drawn, this line would converge with the other lines on the right side of the box at the vanishing point far off to the right.

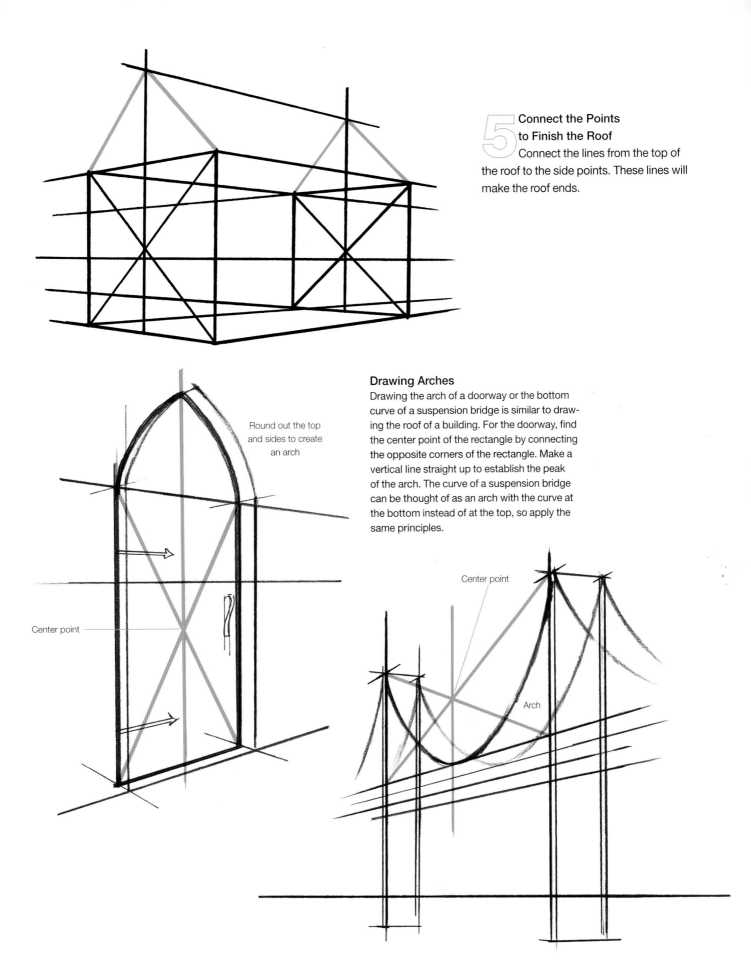

5 Connect the Points to Finish the Roof

Connect the lines from the top of the roof to the side points. These lines will make the roof ends.

Round out the top and sides to create an arch

Center point

Drawing Arches

Drawing the arch of a doorway or the bottom curve of a suspension bridge is similar to drawing the roof of a building. For the doorway, find the center point of the rectangle by connecting the opposite corners of the rectangle. Make a vertical line straight up to establish the peak of the arch. The curve of a suspension bridge can be thought of as an arch with the curve at the bottom instead of at the top, so apply the same principles.

Center point

Arch

Reflections

Reflections are an exciting element to draw because they double the beauty of a scene. The reflection shares the very same horizon and vanishing points as the images they are reflecting.

Reflections Are Perpendicular to Their Reflecting Surface

Reflected images are perpendicular to the reflecting surface. The vertical lines show how both the trees and their reflected images are perpendicular to the surface of the water. This is most noticeable when the reflecting surface is smooth.

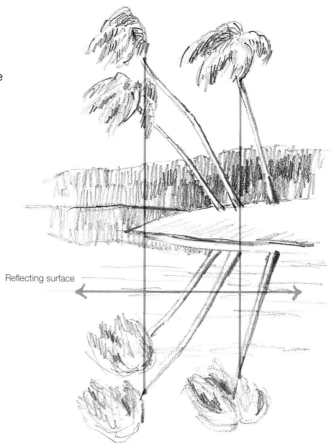

Reflecting surface

Reflections Use the Same Perspective as the Objects They Reflect

In this pond scene, the same horizon and vanishing points are used for both the bridge and its reflection. It is not a repeat or reverse of the bridge, but a continuation.

Vanishing point

Horizon

Reflection on a Rough Surface

When the reflection surface is rough, such as when there are waves on the surface of the water, the reflected image is broken up. This occurs because some of the waves are not perpendicular to the image, causing distortion to the image's reflection.

Distant Elements Can Be Reflected

The image reflected doesn't have to be near or directly over the reflecting surface. The mountains are far away from the water, yet their image is still reflected on its surface.

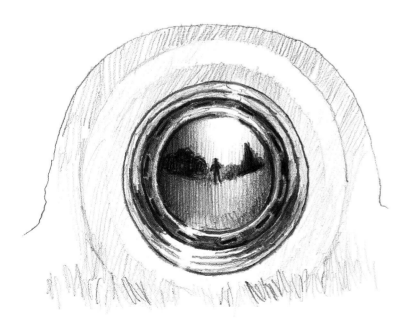

Reflections Can Be a Drawing's Focus

In this example, the reflection on a car's wheel cover shows the sky, ground and trees. Even the person viewing it is visible in the center.

3 Values

Values are the degrees of light and darkness in a drawing. They give additional form and depth to a basic structure. Observing the wide range of values that make up your subject will give you a better understanding of how light creates highlights and shadows on the form.

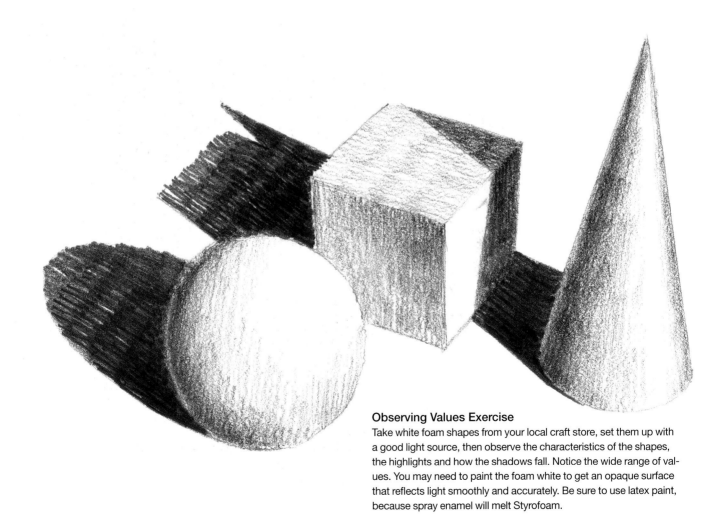

Observing Values Exercise
Take white foam shapes from your local craft store, set them up with a good light source, then observe the characteristics of the shapes, the highlights and how the shadows fall. Notice the wide range of values. You may need to paint the foam white to get an opaque surface that reflects light smoothly and accurately. Be sure to use latex paint, because spray enamel will melt Styrofoam.

Contrast

Differing values create contrasts that can affect the mood and composition of a drawing. The more extreme the difference between values, the greater the contrast. One way to achieve higher contrast in your drawing is to place your darks and lights side by side.

It's All Relative
Value contrasts are relative. They appear differently according to their environment. The small square on the far left may appear darker than the small square on the near left, but both are the same value. The square on the left appears darker because it is placed directly against the pure white of the paper, providing more contrast.

Value Contrast Creates Impact
A drawing done without much contrast will not have much impact and will look flat and pale. The white smoke of the rocket on the right looks brighter against the dark background. The drawing on the right uses richer values, creating more contrast.

You can use a *value scale* to compare the values of a scene with that of a drawing. Hold the value scale up to the subject and look through the holes punched along the side. Where do the values in the subject fall on the value scale? As you begin to compose a drawing (see page 86), it is always best to establish the highlights and very light areas. Sketch those in, then look for where the other values are in the subject. To fill in the other values, one option is to go from the lightest shades of the drawing to the darkest. Another way to map out the values is to fill in some of the darkest areas around the lightest areas, then work with the midtones last. Try each of these methods to see which one works best for you.

Must-Have Materials

4H, HB, 4B graphite pencils
4" × 8" (10cm × 20cm) drawing paper
Kneaded eraser
Hole punch
Scissors
Ruler

1 **Draw a Rectangle**
Draw a 2" × 6" (5cm × 15cm) rectangle on a 4" × 8" (10cm × 20cm) piece of drawing paper. Add a line down the middle right of the rectangle as a guideline for the holes you will punch out in the last step.

2 **Create the Lighter Values**
Keeping the top white, use a 4H pencil to create the lighter values with back-and-forth strokes.

3 **Add the Middle Values**
Add the middle values with an HB pencil.

4 **Add the Darkest Values**
Use a 4B pencil for the darkest values. With scissors, trim around the rectangle pattern you drew, and punch seven holes along one side with a hole punch.

5 **Map Out the Value Variations in Your Reference Photos**
Now you can hold your scale up to a picture or scene to judge the values as you work on your drawings.

Creating Values

When you draw, you use lines to suggest light and dark values. The grade of pencil, the sharpness of its point, the angle of the point on the paper, the amount of pressure applied to the pencil, and the surface of the paper all influence the values you create. Even the pencil strokes you use influence the values you create on the paper.

Often type of stroke and the direction of the lines is determined by the subject. When drawing wood, the pencil lines will follow the direction of the grain; when drawing a cat, the direction of the pencil lines will follow the contours of its body.

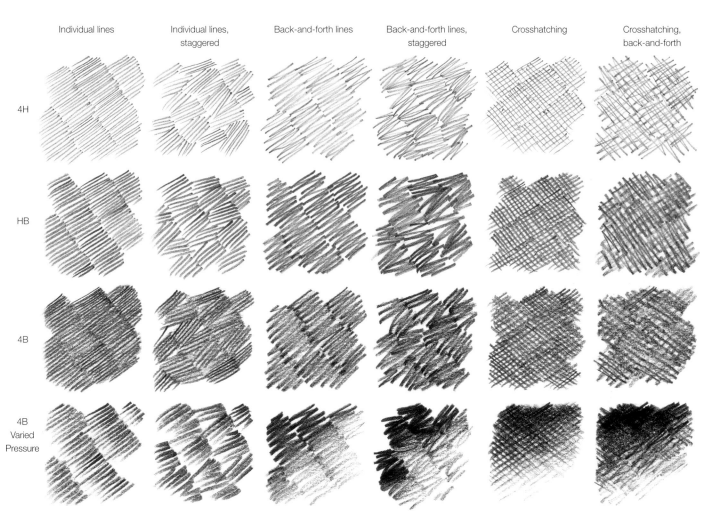

	Individual lines	Individual lines, staggered	Back-and-forth lines	Back-and-forth lines, staggered	Crosshatching	Crosshatching, back-and-forth
4H						
HB						
4B						
4B Varied Pressure						

Different Folks Make Different Strokes

If you are right handed, it is natural for you to make lines moving from the upper right to the lower left. But lines may go any direction you like, depending on what is comfortable for you and the effect you want to achieve.

Making the Grade

Here are some basic lines strokes created with different pencil grades. Hard pencils are good for sharp, crisp line work, and they keep their points longer than soft pencils. Soft-grade pencils can make smooth, dark values. Consider duplicating these pencil strokes as an exercise, then get creative and invent other textures.

Light Effects

Values are used to create the effects of light and shadow in a drawing. To make your drawings look realistic, you will need to replicate these different light effects.

- **Light Source**. Basically, the origin of the light. To determine the shading and shadows of a scene, it is important to determine the position of the *light source* so you know from which direction the light is coming. The light source is usually the sun or a lamp, so the light usually comes from the top. A light source positioned at the top left or right will give more depth than one located straight above your subject.

- **Highlight**. A *highlight* occurs where light reflects off an object. In a drawing, this appears as a bright spot.
- **Form Shadow**. A shadow on an object that gives depth and dimension to its form.
- **Cast Shadow**. A shadow that is cast or thrown by one object onto another surface.
- **Reflected Light**. Light that bounces off a surface and adds light to a region of the object that would otherwise be darker.

Using Light Accurately Adds Realism and Depth to Your Drawings

Light source

Highlight

Form shadow

Cast shadow

Reflected light

An Unnatural Light Source
It's more than just a bad haircut that made Frankenstein's monster look scary. Placing the light source below the subject contributes to his fightening looks.

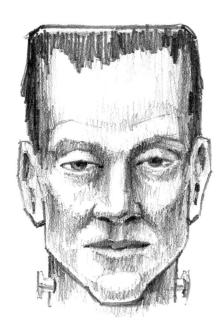

A Natural Light Source
Moving the light source from below the subject to above gives the monster a less frightening appearance.

Plotting Shadows

While the concept of plotting shadows may seem daunting, a basic understanding of it will help you to draw realistically. There are two primary methods of plotting a shadow. One is for when the light source is in the background and can be shown on the drawing; the other is for when the light source is in the foreground and cannot be seen directly. Both of these methods use the principles of linear perspective. You must also plot out the horizon line and vanishing points to be able to get the right perspective for the shape of the object's shadow.

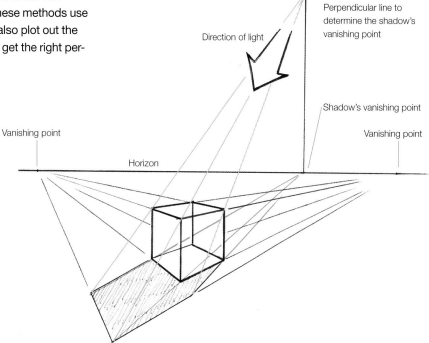

Light Source in the Background

In this example, the light source is in the background. Notice that there is a line coming straight down from the light source to the horizon. That point on the horizon is the shadow's vanishing point. From this vanishing point, draw lines passing through the bottom corners of the cube. Next, draw lines from the light source passing through the top corners of the cube. The intersections between the shadow's vanishing point lines and the light source lines will make the shape of the shadow on the ground.

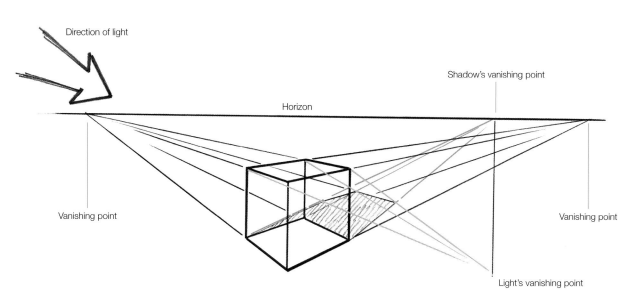

Unseen Light Source in the Foreground

Though the general direction of the light is assumed, the light source is so far away that it cannot be indicated in the drawing. Because of this, the direction of the light and where those lines would converge on the horizon will be a vanishing point. Then draw lines from this vanishing point and pass them through the bottom corners of the cube. Next, plot the lines coming from the vanishing point of the angle of the light source. Place this vanishing point below and perpendicular to the other vanishing point. From this point, draw lines that pass through the top corners of the cube. The intersection of these lines will form the shape of the shadow of the cube.

4 Practice the **Techniques**

You will find certain subjects easier to draw than others. For instance, you may have a knack for drawing faces but feel you can't draw a building in perspective to save your life. When you don't feel comfortable with a certain subject, you will probably try to avoid it, but then you will not gain experience working with that subject. Challenge yourself—give some of the lessons you may deem more difficult a chance. You might even try some lessons more than once, then compare the results from your first attempt with your last. I predict that you will be amazed at the improvement in your drawing skills. You can draw all of these examples with your 4H, HB and 4B pencils. Use the 4H and HB pencils for the light and medium values and the 4B pencil for the darkest values.

Drawing Subjects Are Everywhere
Be on the lookout for drawing subjects such as these rocks. This drawing was done from a photograph taken by one of my students, Jackie Chunko.

Study of Rocks
Graphite on drawing paper
11" × 14" (28cm × 36cm)

Clouds and Grass

The world around us offers an infinite number of subjects to draw. Commonplace items such as clouds and grass can be interesting by themselves or as complements to other elements in a picture.

When drawing clouds, start by sketching the outline, but use subtle value changes to show the shape and depth of their forms. You can achieve value changes by varying the type or pressure of your pencil strokes. Be particularly conscious of the location of your light source. Stormy days while the sun is still out are especially good for drawing clouds because there are so many sharp contrasts between the lights and darks of the sky.

Clouds in Sunlight
With the light source above, the tops of the clouds appear lighter, while the undersides appear darker and shadowed. One way to learn how to draw clouds in sunlight is to study the effects of light on something more solid, such as cotton balls.

Clouds Blocking the Sunlight
Clouds can be both translucent and opaque. When the light source is behind the clouds, the cloud in front of the sun will appear bright white around the thin, translucent edges where the light shines through it. The thicker parts of the cloud will appear darker because they are more opaque, blocking more of the light.

Grass in Sunlight
Line strokes can imply individual blades of grass. Use darker strokes to indicate shading and depth.

Grass in Sunlight and Shadow
The background grass is shown as a dark silhouette, whereas the foreground grass is suggested with light pencil strokes. Vary the direction and spacing of the lines to make the grass look more interesting.

Leafy Trees

Trees may be the center of interest in a scene or just a background element. Each tree has a character all its own.

CHECK THIS OUT

Holding the Pencil (p. 15) Creating Values (p. 51)
Using Basic Shapes (p. 27)

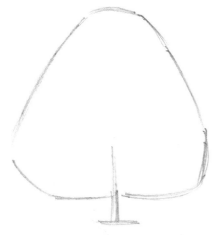

1 Sketch the Basic Shape
Start with the basic overall shape of the tree. Place the trunk toward the bottom of the page.

2 Sketch the Branches and Refine the Shape
Sketch in some of the branches. Even if the branches are not visible in the final drawing, sketching them will help you understand both the structure of the tree and the placement of the leaves. Add more definition to the outer form of the tree by outlining the edges of the leaves.

Branch Out

Exposed branches can add interest to an otherwise ordinary tree. First sketch the branches of the tree, then erase the lines that are going to be covered by the leaves. Finally, shade in the leaves.

3 Add the Leaves and Shading
Erase any unnecessary lines. Use a variety of back-and-forth lines to suggest the leaves. Make some lines darker than others to create shadows. Notice that the direction of the lines adds a sense of liveliness to an otherwise static subject. Remove your initial outline with an eraser.

Evergreen Trees

Use the same basic steps to draw evergreens as you would use to draw leafy trees. When drawing a tree, examine the subject closely to capture its uniqueness.

CHECK THIS OUT

Holding the Pencil (p. 15)   Creating Values (p. 51)
Using Basic Shapes (p. 27)

Must-Have Materials

Graphite pencil
Drawing board
Drawing paper
Kneaded eraser

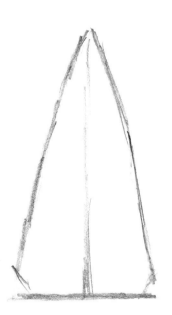

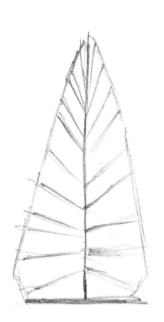

1 Sketch the Basic Shape
Start with the basic overall shape and trunk.

2 Sketch the Branches
Sketch in the branches, noticing their direction. The branches angle downward the farther down you place them on the tree. Many trees are structured like this, not only evergreens.

3 Add the Needles and Shading
Erase any unnecessary lines. Use a variety of staggered back-and-forth lines to suggest the needles of the tree. Apply some lines more heavily than others to create shading and depth.

Carry a Camera

Be on the lookout for interesting trees that you can photograph and use as references for future drawings.

Brick, Stone and Wood

Knowing how to draw different building materials such as brick, stone and wood comes in handy when you want to draw a house. These elements add a range of textures that make your drawing more interesting. Besides, they're fun to draw.

Bricks Up Close

A subject viewed up close will display more texture than when viewed from a distance, so it should be drawn differently to show that detail. To emphasize their worn appearance, draw old bricks with multidirectional lines of varied degrees of thickness.

Bricks at a Distance

A distant view of bricks is drawn with minimal detail. Use back-and-forth line strokes to add values to the bricks. Add shadows under the individual bricks with heavy dark lines for a subtle sense of depth. Also create depth through the use of one-point perspective.

Fitted Stones

Draw the massive fitted stones of an ancient Roman building with shading lines going in different directions to show texture. Make the joints of the stones dark to imply shadow and depth.

Rough Stones

Use irregular shapes and sizes, varied line strokes and shading to create a wall of rough stones. Add heavy, dark lines under the stones to imply shadow and depth. Notice the left end of the wall is set against a background made of dark vertical line strokes to suggest a corner.

Wood Beams

Draw wood grain using differing values and line strokes. Make the places where the wood was chipped out darker to suggest shadow and depth. Use semicircular lines to create the knots in the boards.

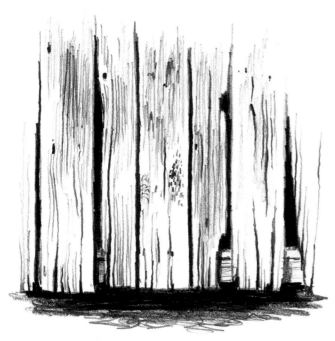

Wood Boards

Draw weathered wood boards with coarse pencil strokes flowing in similar directions to show the grain. The spaces underneath and between the boards are dark to suggest depth.

Rocks

MINI DEMONSTRATION

Apply the same drawing principles and techniques that are used when drawing complex subjects to relatively simple subjects such as rocks. You can make the drawing more interesting by varying the shapes and sizes of the rocks.

CHECK THIS OUT

Holding the Pencil (p. 15)
Using Basic Shapes (p. 27)
Gauging Proportions (p. 28)

Creating Values (p. 51)
Light Effects (p. 52)

Must-Have Materials

Graphite pencil
Drawing board
Drawing paper
Kneaded eraser

1 **Sketch the Basic Shapes**
Sketch the outer shapes of the rocks, varying the sizes and shapes for interest.

2 **Map Out the Lights and Darks**
Add lines to map out the lights and darks on the rocks. In this case, the light comes from the upper right, so draw lines on the upper right areas of the rocks for the highlights and on the lower left areas for the darkest portions of the rocks.

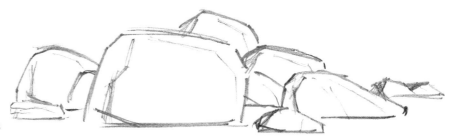

3 **Add Shading and Shadows**
Use consistent up-and-down pencil strokes so that the surface of the rocks will look smooth. Make the pencil strokes darker on the left side of the rocks to create shading and depth.

Other Types of Rocks

You may think that if you've seen one rock you've seen them all, but that just isn't true. Rocks offer a variety of shapes, sizes and textures.

Coarse Rocks
The rough shaping of these rocks makes each one unique. This appears to be a simple drawing, but its subtle value changes make it challenging The outer shape of some of the background rocks is defined by the shading behind them.

Projecting Rocks
These rocks jut upward, their top edges appearing light in value. Use back-and-forth lines to fill in the values, altering the pressure of some of the strokes to add shading and depth.

CHECK THIS OUT

Holding the Pencil (p. 15)
Using a Frisket (p. 15)
Using an Erasing Shield (p. 18)
Gauging Proportions (p. 28)

Two-Point Perspective (p. 36)
Ellipses (p. 42)
Creating Values (p. 51)
Light Effects (p. 52)

Must-Have Materials

Graphite pencil
Drawing board
Drawing paper
Kneaded eraser

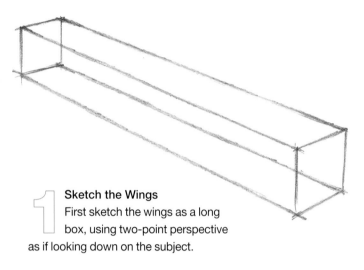

1 Sketch the Wings
First sketch the wings as a long box, using two-point perspective as if looking down on the subject.

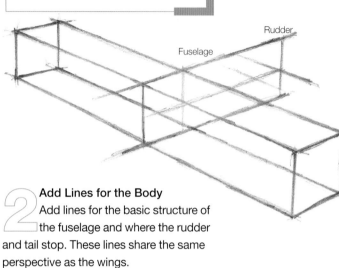

2 Add Lines for the Body
Add lines for the basic structure of the fuselage and where the rudder and tail stop. These lines share the same perspective as the wings.

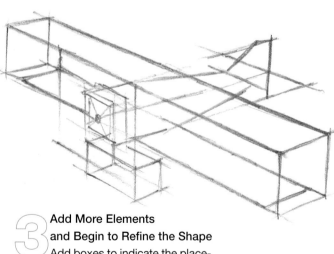

3 Add More Elements and Begin to Refine the Shape
Add boxes to indicate the placement of the wheels and engine area. Draw lines to better define the shapes of the rudder. Chisel out the fuselage and shorten the lower wing tips.

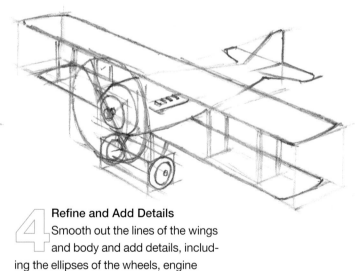

4 Refine and Add Details
Smooth out the lines of the wings and body and add details, including the ellipses of the wheels, engine compartment and propeller.

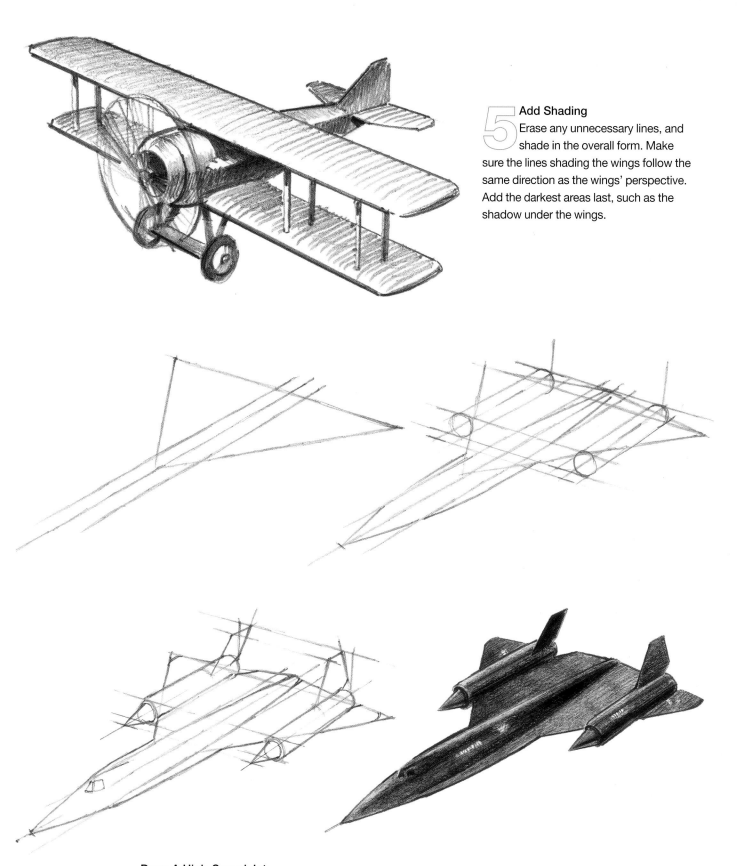

5 Add Shading

Erase any unnecessary lines, and shade in the overall form. Make sure the lines shading the wings follow the same direction as the wings' perspective. Add the darkest areas last, such as the shadow under the wings.

Draw A High-Speed Jet

First draw the basic shapes in perspective to carve out the shape of the plane. Add highlights, shadows and details.

Train

This type of steam engine is a Norfolk and Western 4-8-4. The structural elements of this scene are drawn using one-point perspective. Make use of the principles of atmospheric perspective as you apply the lights and darks. When you want to shade subjects like these, friskets and erasing shields may be handy tools to use.

Must-Have Materials

Graphite pencil
Drawing board
Drawing paper
Kneaded eraser

CHECK THIS OUT

Holding the Pencil (p. 15)
Using a Frisket (p. 15)
Using an Erasing Shield (p. 18)
Gauging Proportions (p. 28)

One-Point Perspective (p. 34)
Atmospheric Perspective (p. 41)
Creating Values (p. 51)

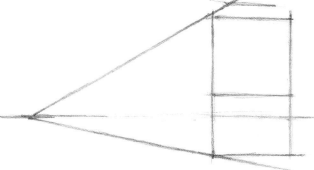

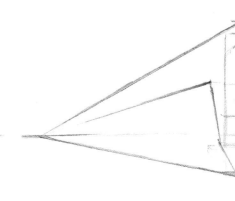

1 Sketch the Basic Shapes
Draw the horizon line, with the vanishing point on the left side. Start with the basic shape in one-point perspective. Notice that all the vertical lines are perpendicular to the horizon at this stage.

2 Indicate the Basic Shapes of the Front
Fill the previously drawn square with a circle. Add other lines to indicate the basic shaping of the front of the engine.

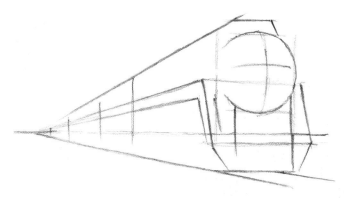

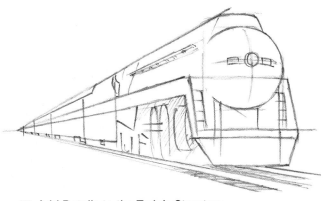

3 Add More Structural Lines
Add the more obvious lines, including the vertical lines that define the individual cars. Add a cross in the upper middle of the circle, to mark the placement of the engine lights.

4 Add Details to the Train's Structure
Add the tracks, wheels, engine light and smaller details such as the handrail and the steps. Also add trim to the tops of the cars.

5 Add Shading

Erase any unnecessary lines, and finish with shading. Use uniform up-and-down pencil strokes to make a smooth appearance. Create atmospheric perspective by drawing the closer portion of the train with more contrasts and details than the more distant portion.

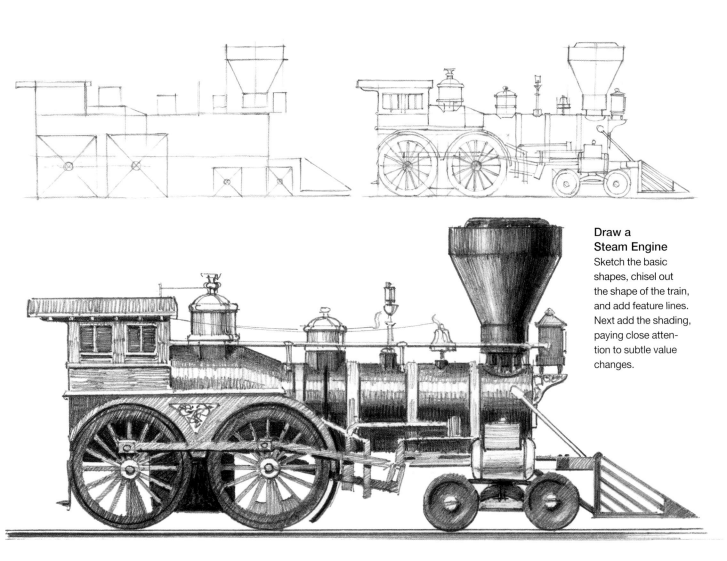

Draw a Steam Engine

Sketch the basic shapes, chisel out the shape of the train, and add feature lines. Next add the shading, paying close attention to subtle value changes.

Automobile

This is a Facel Vega, a French sports car built in the 1950s and 1960s. This is a fun lesson to practice dissecting your subjects by first looking for the basic shapes, remembering the rules of perspective.

CHECK THIS OUT

Holding the Pencil (p. 15)
Gauging Proportions (p. 28)
Two-Point Perspective (p. 36)

Ellipses (p. 42)
Creating Values (p. 51)

Must-Have Materials

Graphite pencil
Drawing board
Drawing paper
Kneaded eraser

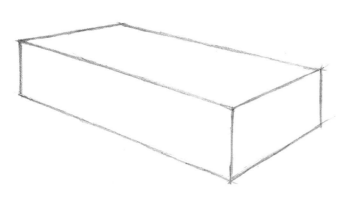

1 Sketch the Basic Shapes
Sketch a basic box shape in two-point perspective. Take the time to get this right so the rest of the drawing will work out accurately.

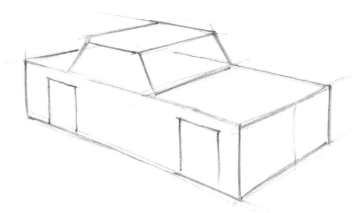

2 Add the Top and Squares for the Wheels
Add the top of the car to the basic shape. Draw squares in perspective to indicate the wheels' placement. This will help you draw the ellipses for the tires accurately. Like all the elements, the squares share the same perspective as the basic box shape.

3 Add and Refine the Structural Lines
Chisel out the shape of the car, and sketch in ellipses for the wheels. Add lines to mark the placement of the front elements such as the grill and headlights.

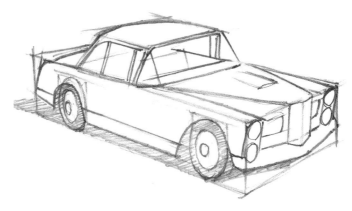

4 Add Details and Begin Shading
Add details such as the headlights, grill, windows and interior. Keep in mind that the cutouts for the wheel are shaped differently from the wheels themselves. Add some shading to the wheels and shadow under the car.

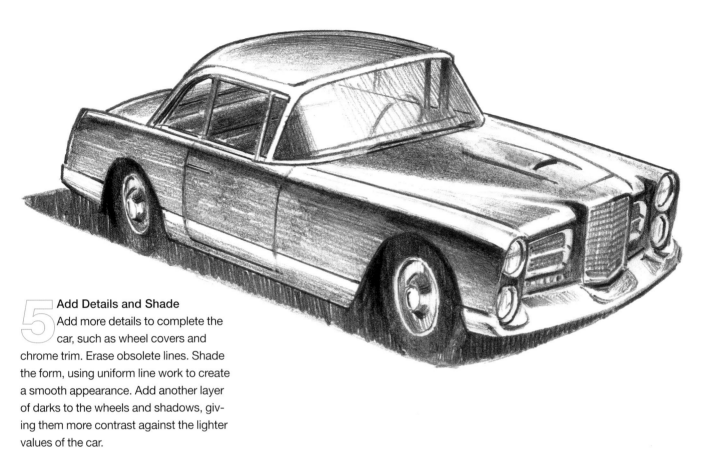

5 Add Details and Shade

Add more details to complete the car, such as wheel covers and chrome trim. Erase obsolete lines. Shade the form, using uniform line work to create a smooth appearance. Add another layer of darks to the wheels and shadows, giving them more contrast against the lighter values of the car.

Creating a Shiny, Metallic Surface

Rich darks and graduated values give this Jaguar a shiny metallic appearance. It is important to make uniform pencil lines to create the smooth, metallic look for the car's surface.

MINI DEMONSTRATION

The graceful lines of boats and shimmering water reflections inspire great compositions. For this demonstration, we'll start with a simple side view.

CHECK THIS OUT

Holding the Pencil (p. 15)   Gauging Proportions (p. 28)

Using Basic Shapes (p. 27)   Locating Vanishing Points (p. 40)

1 Sketch the the Lines of the Hull
Start with the lines of the hull, which tilt slightly upward on the left side.

2 Finish the Basic Shape of the Hull and Indicate the Cabin
Connect the ends to complete the basic shape of the hull. Add lines to indicate the placement of the cabin.

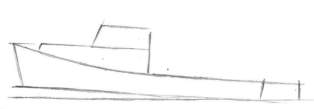

3 Add the Side of the Cabin and the Top of the Hull
Draw the side of the cabin and the curve of the top of the hull. The boat is viewed from the side and at a distance, making it look flat.

4 Add Details
Sketch in details, including windows, trim and the man.

5 Shade to Finish
Add values to the elements. Use long, straight pencil strokes on the hull. Make the inside of the cabin dark.

Sketch a Rowboat
Sketch the basic shapes in perspective, then add details and shading.

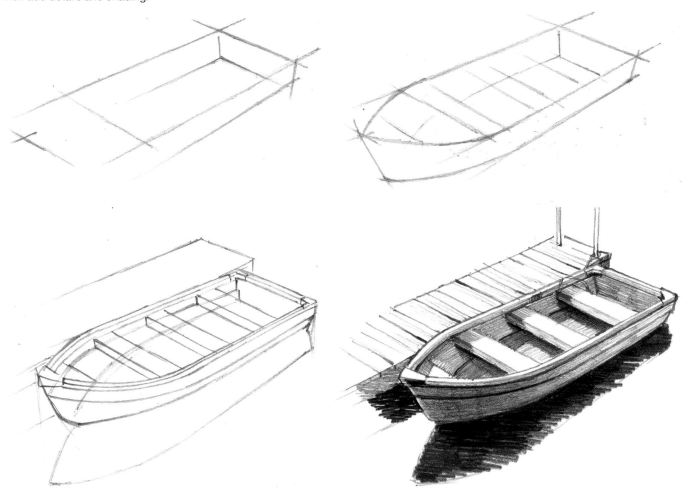

Cat Face

For those of you who are cat lovers, this demo will be lots of fun. For those of you who prefer dogs (we know everyone falls under one of the two categories), go ahead and try this exercise, then give the finished art to one of your cat-loving friends. This demo offers a great way to develop your shading skills.

CHECK THIS OUT

Holding the Pencil (p. 15)
Using Basic Shapes (p. 27)
Gauging Proportions (p. 28)
Creating Values (p. 51)

Must-Have Materials

Graphite pencil
Drawing board
Drawing paper
Kneaded eraser

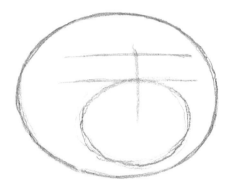

1 Sketch the Basic Shapes
To draw the feline face, start with the basic outer oval, two lines for the top and bottom of the eyes, and an oval for the snout.

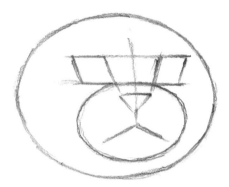

2 Place the Facial Elements
Add more lines for the eyes, mouth and the top of the ears, as well as a triangle for the nose.

3 Add the Ears and Neck
Add lines to indicate the ears and neck.

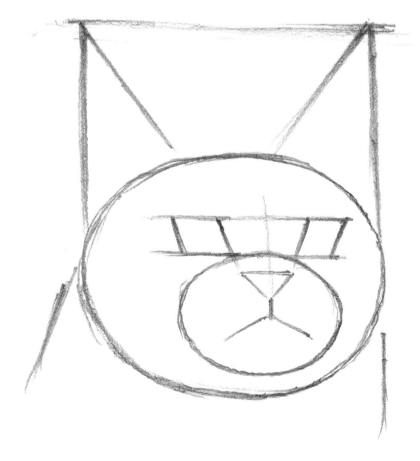

4 **Refine the Lines and Add Details**
Refine the structural lines, rounding and curving where necessary. Add details, including the pupils, nose and muzzle.

5 **Add Shading**
Erase any obsolete lines. Add shading with pencil strokes that follow the direction of the fur. Apply darker values for the stripes and shadows.

Side View of a Cat

Cats are as varied as people, and it is fun to capture their unique qualities in your drawings. In addition to helping you create shape and texture, this demo will give you an opportunity to work on developing your proportioning skills. To sketch the legs and body in the correct proportions, first sketch a *baseline*. A baseline is used to establish the placement of your subject and to help work out proportions of a drawing.

Must-Have Materials

Graphite pencil
Drawing board
Drawing paper
Kneaded eraser

CHECK THIS OUT

Holding the Pencil (p. 15)
Using Basic Shapes (p. 27)
Gauging Proportions (p. 28)
Creating Values (p. 51)

1 Sketch the Basic Body Shape
Draw a rectangle to suggest the basic body structure. Take the vertical lines all the way down to the baseline.

2 Add the Head Shape
Sketch an oval for the head. Position it so it just overlaps the top horizontal line.

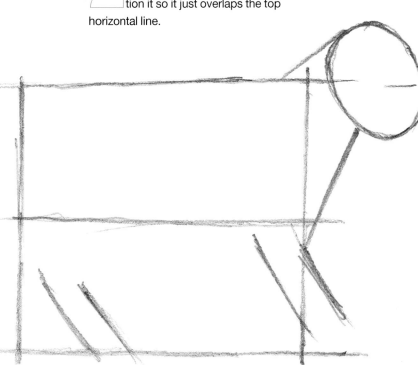

3 Add the Neck and Legs
Add lines for the neck that connect the head to the body. Sketch angled lines for the legs. See page 30 for instructions on how to transfer angles.

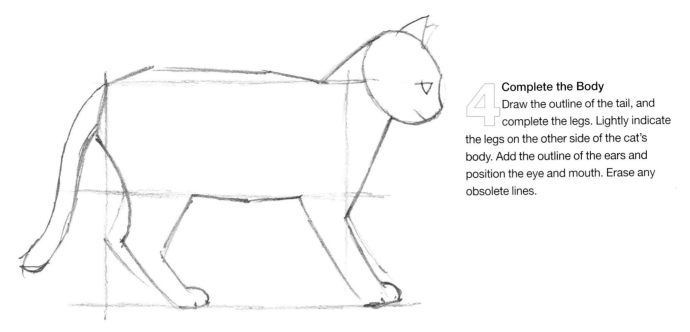

Complete the Body

4 Draw the outline of the tail, and complete the legs. Lightly indicate the legs on the other side of the cat's body. Add the outline of the ears and position the eye and mouth. Erase any obsolete lines.

Add the Shading and Details

5 Use back-and-forth strokes to suggest the cat's fur, varying the lights and darks to imply form. Add details to the eye, mouth, nose, ear and paws.

Side View of a Dog

Use the steps you practiced on the cat's body (see page 72) to draw a dachshund. Start with the basic overall structure and then add more features as your drawing progresses. While observing dachshunds for this drawing, I became aware of how short dachshunds really are!

CHECK THIS OUT

Holding the Pencil (p. 15)   Gauging Proportions (p. 28)

Using Basic Shapes (p. 27)   Creating Values (p. 51)

Must-Have Materials
Graphite pencil
Drawing board
Drawing paper
Kneaded eraser

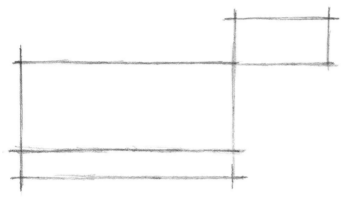

1 Sketch the Basic Shapes
Sketch lines to form the basic body and head structure, including a baseline to establish where the feet will rest.

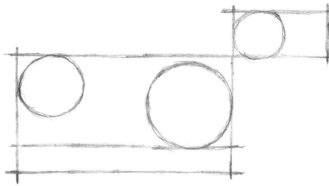

2 Add Circles for the Head and Body
Add circles for the head, chest and rear. This will help you shape the dog's overall form.

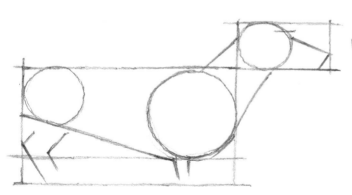

3 Add Lines for the Body, Neck and Legs
Connect the circles to form the shape of the body and neck. Sketch lines that will indicate the muzzle and the foreground legs.

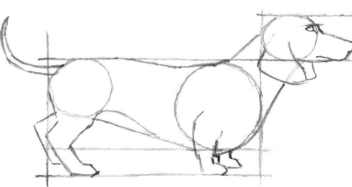

4 Refine Lines and Add Structural Details
Refine the line work to further shape the dog's body. Add the eye, tail, ears and legs. Place the background legs so they are staggered in comparison to the foreground legs.

5 **Add Fur, Details and Shading** Erase any obsolete lines. Shade the dog's glossy coat with short, uniform pencil strokes that follow the fur's direction. Add details to the eye, nose, mouth and paws.

Drawing Long Fur

Use long pencil strokes that follow the direction of the fur to shade in the coat for a longhaired dog. Make these pencil strokes less uniform than those used for a shorthaired dog. This will make the long fur look more textured.

Cows are incredible creatures. Besides giving us milk, cheese and meat, cows do amazing tricks, but no one knows about it because they pull these stunts only when no one is looking.

CHECK THIS OUT

Holding the Pencil (p. 15)   Gauging Proportions (p. 28)
Using Basic Shapes (p. 27)   Creating Values (p. 51)

Must-Have Materials

Graphite pencil
Drawing board
Drawing paper
Kneaded eraser

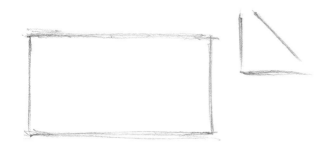

1 Sketch the Basic Shapes
Sketch the basic shapes: a rectangle for the body and a triangle for the head. Add a baseline to establish the length of the legs.

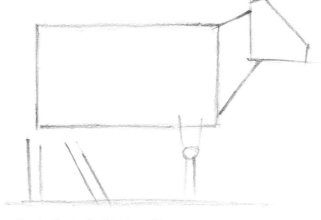

2 Indicate the Neck and Legs
Add lines for the neck and legs. Pay attention to the placement and angles of these lines. Use a small circle to indicate the joint of the front knee.

3 Refine the Lines
Refine the line work to further shape the cow's body. Add the eye, ears, tail and udders.

4 Add Shading and Finishing Details
Erase any extra lines. Add light shading to imply form, using darker shading in the more shadowed places. Make the coat's dark patches with semi-uniform back-and-forth pencil strokes.

Swan
MINI DEMONSTRATION

The elegant lines of this swan makes it an interesting subject. Enjoy practicing your skills with this mini demo and then consider using your drawing as a greeting card.

CHECK THIS OUT

Holding the Pencil (p. 15)

Using Basic Shapes (p. 27)

Measuring Proportions (p. 28)

Creating Values (p. 51)

Must-Have Materials

Graphite pencil

Drawing board

Drawing paper

Kneaded eraser

1 Sketch the Basic Shapes
Sketch the basic shapes of the head and body. Be conscious of their proportions and placement.

2 Add the Neck and Beak
Add curved lines for the neck, then add the beak, paying attention to the distance between the neck lines.

3 Sketch in the Feathers
Indicate the feather placement on the swan's back, and add the eye to the head.

4 Add Final Details and Shading
Add the shading with short pencil strokes. Start with the lighter values, then add another layer of pencil strokes for the darker areas.

Human Figures

People make fascinating subjects to draw. While at a mall, just look at all the different sizes, shapes and proportions of the people around you. Though you may observe that people come in many different "varieties," there are basic principles that apply to all humans.

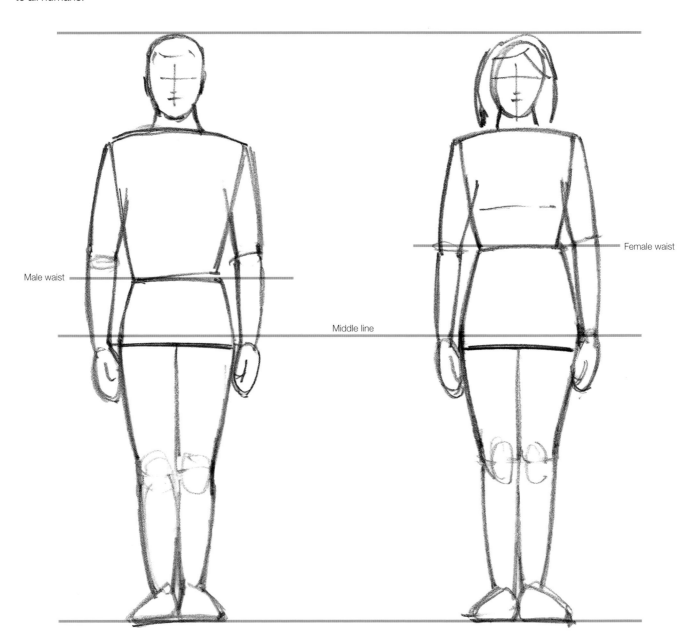

Male waist

Female waist

Middle line

Proportions for Adults
Though men are generally taller than women, they are shown as the same height here for comparison. For both sexes, almost half the height is made up of the legs, with the tips of the hands falling to the mid-thigh region. The waist is lower in men than in women. Another difference is that men are generally bulkier and wider than women.

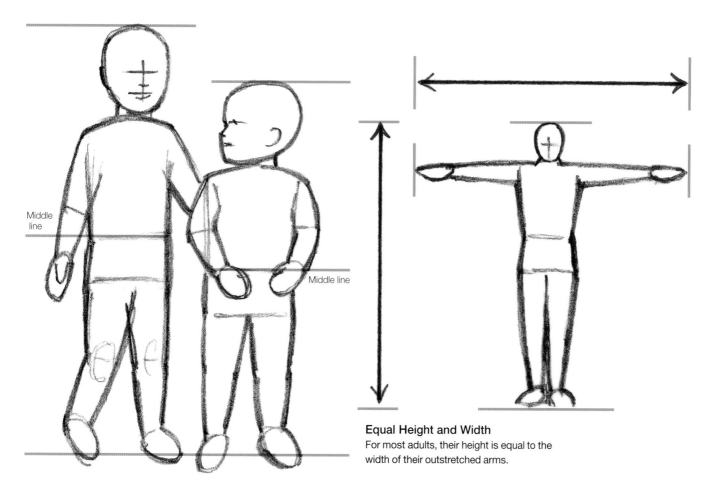

Middle line

Middle line

Equal Height and Width
For most adults, their height is equal to the width of their outstretched arms.

Proportions for Children
Children are proportioned differently from adults, more noticeably in younger children. Their bodies are smaller in relation to their heads, and their legs are shorter, with the tops of their legs well below the middle line.

Figure Drawing
Once you become familiar with basic body structure and proportions, you can draw more confidently, using a minimum of structural guidelines.

Structural Sketch
This sketch has its structural elements blocked in.

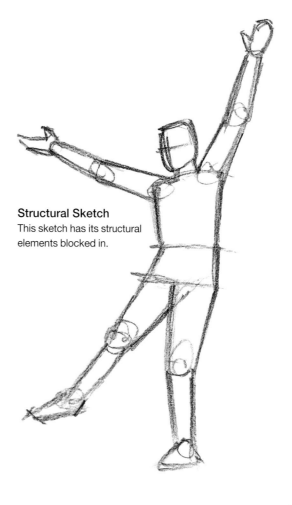

Man Standing

DEMONSTRATION

As you draw the human figure, remember that almost half the height of the body is the legs. Establish the middle line first, then mark the top of the inseam. Pay attention to the head size, which takes up a little more than one-eighth of the overall height. A common mistake in figure drawing is to make the head too large and the legs too short.

CHECK THIS OUT

Holding the Pencil (p. 15)
Using Basic Shapes (p. 27)
Gauging Poportions (p. 28)
Creating Values (p. 51)

Must-Have Materials

Graphite pencil
Drawing board
Drawing paper
Kneaded eraser

1 Establish the General Proportions
Start with lines to indicate the placement and proportions. Because the weight of the body in this example rests over the man's right leg, include a vertical line that goes from the head to the right foot.

Add top, bottom and middle horizontal lines. Then sketch a line halfway between the middle and top lines, then sketch another line between the last line drawn and the top line.

2 Sketch the Head and Legs
Most adults are about 7½ heads high. The distance from the top line to the next lower line is one-eighth of the overall height. Make a line slightly lower and sketch an egg shape for the head, which should work out to about 7½ units of the overall height. You can use dividers if you want to check your proportions. Sketch in the legs, placing the top of the inseam just below the middle line.

3 **Add the Torso and Waist**
Sketch the basic shape of the torso along with the waistline.

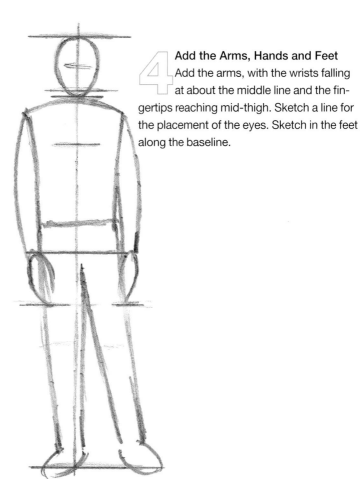

4 **Add the Arms, Hands and Feet**
Add the arms, with the wrists falling at about the middle line and the fingertips reaching mid-thigh. Sketch a line for the placement of the eyes. Sketch in the feet along the baseline.

5 **Sketch in Details**
Sketch in the details, including facial features and clothes.

6 **Shade the Drawing**
Add shading and details.

Face: Front View
MINI DEMONSTRATION

To draw faces correctly, it's important to understand their basic structures and proportions. One way to do this is to use the width of the eye as a unit of measurement. These examples show generic proportions of an adult male of European origin. The features of individuals vary according to age, gender and ethnicity, if only in subtle ways.

1 **Sketch the Basic Shape**
Start with the basic shape egg-shape of the head. It should be five eye-widths wide by seven eye-widths high.

2 **Add the Eye Line**
Sketch a horizontal line in the middle of the face to place the eyes. Sketch a vertical line to establish the center of the face.

3 **Add Eye Shapes and Nose and Mouth Lines**
Sketch the eyes, leaving one eye-width between them. Add a line for the nose a little less than half the distance from the eyes to the chin. Sketch a line for the mouth a little less than halfway between the line for the nose and chin.

4 **Add Eyebrows and Lips**
Add a horizontal line above the eyes for the eyebrows and sketch them in. Add the top and bottom lips.

5 **Add the Nose and Ears**
Add the base of the nose. The width of the nose aligns with the inside corners of the eyes. Add the ears, with the tops of the ears aligned with the eyebrows and the bottoms aligned with the base of the nose.

6 **Add Details**
Add details to the eyes and nose, along with the hair and neck.

General Face Proportions

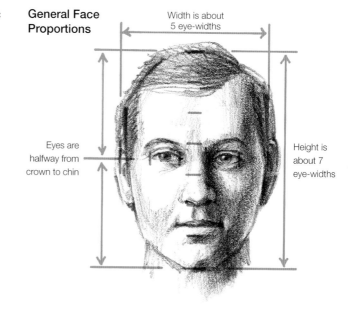

Width is about 5 eye-widths

Eyes are halfway from crown to chin

Height is about 7 eye-widths

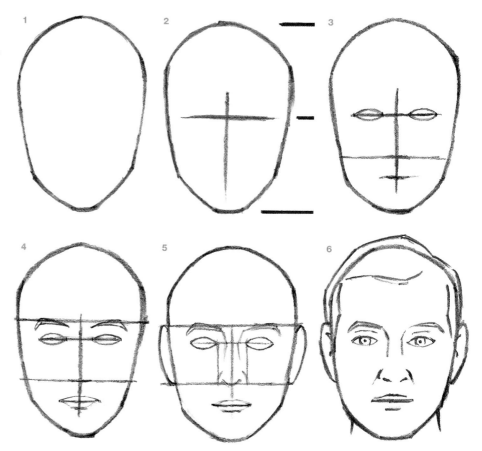

Face: Three-Quarters View

A three-quarters view of the face shows most of the face and part of the side of the head. Keep in mind that the proportions and the placement of the elements are similar to the front view.

Must-Have Materials
Graphite pencil
Drawing board
Drawing paper
Kneaded eraser

1 Sketch the Basic Shape
Sketch an egg-shape for the three-quarters view with the chin slightly off-center toward the right.

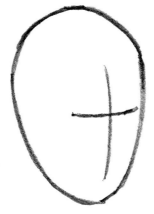

2 Add the Eye Line
Add a slightly off-center horizontal line for the eyes. Sketch a vertical line through the middle of the eye line to establish the center of the face.

3 Add Eye Shapes and Lines for the Nose and Mouth
Sketch the shapes of the eyes with one eye-width between them. Add a line for the nose a little less than half the distance from the eyes to the chin. Sketch a line for the mouth a little less than half the distance between the line for the nose and the chin.

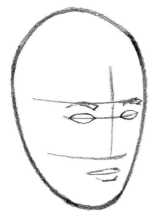

4 Add Eyebrows and Lips
Add a line to place the eyebrows, then sketch in the eyebrows. The curve of the brows should follow the curve of the eyes. Add the top and bottom lips.

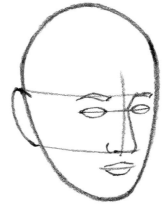

5 Add the Nose and Ear
Add the nose. Working down, the nose bridge should angle in toward the center of the eyes and then angle out from the center to the base of the nose. Add the ear, with the top aligning with the eyebrows and the bottom aligning with the nose's base.

6 Add Details
Add details to the eyes and nose, along with the hair and neck.

Face: Side View

Placing the elements for a side view of a face is similar to that for the front and three-quarters view. As with all drawings, look for proportions and places where the elements align. You may want to examine the proportions with a tool such as a pencil, dividers or a sewing gauge (see page 28).

Must-Have Materials

Graphite pencil
Drawing board
Drawing paper
Kneaded eraser

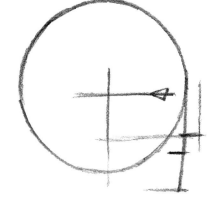

1 Sketch the Basic Shapes
Sketch a circle for the top and middle portion of the head. Sketch a vertical line down from the right side of the circle for the front of the face. Add a short horizontal line at the end of the vertical line, slightly lower than the circle, as the base of the chin.

2 Add Lines for the Eye, Nose and Ear
Sketch a horizontal line, halfway between the top of the chin, the circle and the base of the chin, for the placement of the eye. Sketch a vertical line to the right of the circle to help with the placement of the nose. Another vertical line, coming from the center of the circle, will help with the placement of the ear.

3 Add the Eye Shape and Lines for the Nose and Mouth
Sketch a triangle for the eye, placing it about a third of the distance from the right edge of the circle to the vertical line for the ear. Sketch a horizontal line a little less than half the distance from the eye line to the chin line for the base of the ear. Add a short horizontal line a little less than half the distance from the previously established nose line to the chin line to help place the mouth.

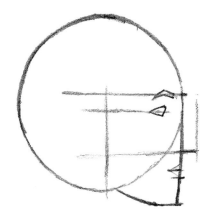

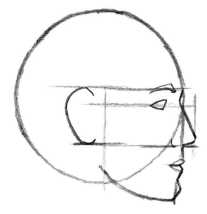

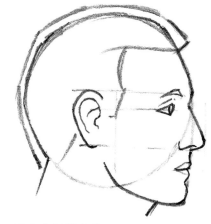

4 Add Eyebrows and Lips
Add a horizontal line for the eyebrow. Sketch the eyebrow, making it slightly curved. Add lines for the lips, connecting them to the vertical line in the front of the face.

5 Add the Ear and Form the Profile
Sketch the ear shape, placing it slightly left of the central vertical line and from the brow line to the nose baseline. Form the profile of the face and complete the jawline, which ends near the lower right part of the ear.

6 Add Details
Add details to the eyes, ears and nose. Add the hair and neck.

Drawing Individual Faces

Most adult faces have similar overall proportions, with the differences being most noticeable in the features such as the eyes, nose, ears and lips.

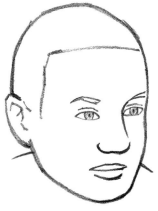

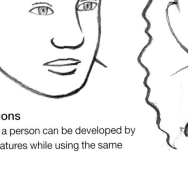

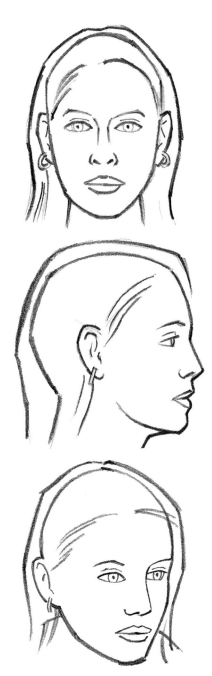

Ethnic Variations
The ethnicity of a person can be developed by changing the features while using the same basic structure.

Age Variations
For an elderly man or woman, draw the ears and nose larger, the chin longer and make noticeable wrinkles.

Child's Face
The proportions of a child's face are different from those of an adult. While the eyes of an adult are placed at the middle, a child's eyes are below the middle, creating a bigger forehead. The head itself is wide and the features small.

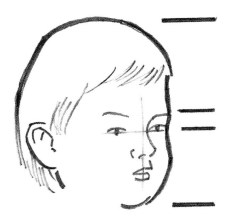

Women's Features
When drawing a woman's face, follow the same basic proportions and placement of features as used for the generic male. The ears, nose and jawline are usually smaller and more delicate, the lips larger and more noticeable. Details such as earrings, eyeliner and hairstyle can also express femininity.

5 Composition

Composition involves the arrangement of the elements in an artwork. Though composition is inherent to all art, good composition involves planning and forethought. A strong composition entertains the viewer, while a weak composition may make the viewer feel indifferent toward the artwork. A good composition is cleverly planned to lead the viewer through the scene.

Aspects of composition include symmetry, the number and placement of elements within the scene, and how the scene is framed. As you plan your composition, you will also decide on a format, create a path for the viewer's eye, and look for trouble spots.

The Old Tractor
Graphite on drawing paper
11" × 14" (28cm × 36cm)

Arranging the Elements

Symmetrical composition can be useful if you want to make your subject look orderly and structured, but it often comes across as bland. *Asymmetrical* composition is preferable because it makes the objects in your drawing seem more neutral.

Symmetrical Composition
Though this scene is evenly balanced, it has two strikes against it: the horizontal line splits the scene exactly in half, and because the tree is placed in the middle of the composition, the scene looks contrived.

Asymmetrical Composition
Moving the tree off center makes the scene asymmetrical. The viewer should find this more appealing and realistic.

Using a Grid for Asymmetrical Composition
One method for achieving balance in an asymmetrical composition is to divide the picture into nine equal rectangles. Use the intersections of these gridlines to locate major elements in the scene.

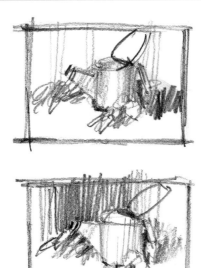

Using Thumbnail Sketches

Thumbnail sketches allow you to plan what the finished drawing will look like. Examine the differing placement of lights and darks in these examples. Can you tell which thumbnail sketch was used as a guide for the Textured Metal demonstration (page 94)?

Number of Elements

The number and placement of elements can affect the balance of the composition and by leading the viewer through the scene. An odd number is usually more interesting than an even number. Evens and odds can also refer to the number of elements reaching the edge of the artwork, which affects the way the viewer's eye travels in and out of the composition.

Even Number of Elements
An even number of elements can seem uninteresting. The viewer's eye has nowhere to go but from one fish to the other.

Odd Number of Elements
An odd number of elements is usually more interesting than an even number. This scene has an odd number of elements, with one dominant and two subordinate elements. The viewer is first drawn to the big fish, then to the smaller fish, then back to the big fish.

Even Number of Elements at the Edge
Evens and odds can also refer to the number of elements that reach the edge of the artwork. In this example, the buildings are touching the edge on the left and the right, making an even number.

Odd Number of Elements at the Edge
A simple change allows the buildings to touch the edge on the left, right and top, creating a more interesting composition.

Cropping and Formatting

Some scenes contain too much visual information to include in a composition, and it can be hard to determine where to begin and what to leave out. By looking through a *viewfinder*, you can visually *crop* the composition before you pick up the pencil. Once you have determined the area you want to include, you will find the drawing easier to manage.

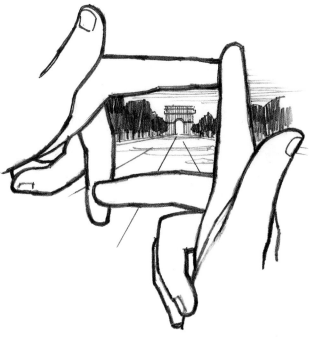

Using a Viewfinder
One method for planning a composition is to crop the scene with a viewfinder, a piece of cardboard with a cutout like a window frame. This is especially helpful when working outdoors, when the subject may seem overwhelming and you don't know where to focus your attention.

Using Your Fingers
Forming a rectangle with your fingers is another way to crop a scene without using any special equipment.

Format Affects a Composition's Mood
The mood of a picture can be accentuated by its overall shape, or *format*. A horizontal format tends to give a stable, more serene feel, while a vertical format can feel more impressive or powerful.

Add Diagonals to Your Subject
Diagonal lines and angled elements create a sense of action in a drawing.

Lines, Tangents and Shapes

Leading lines guide the viewer through a composition. Lines can be indicated through a pattern of elements, such as stepping stones that lead the viewer to another place in the composition. Leading lines can also guide the viewer to a *focal point*, which is the center of interest in a composition.

In art, a *tangent* is the unfortunate meeting of two or more similar lines or elements. Artists usually avoid tangents because they can make a scene confusing.

Good Use of Leading Lines
In this example we are led back to the distant mountains.

Tangents Cause Confusion
Tangents can be confusing for a viewer. This sketch has a tangent where the tree aligns with the end of the house, making it look as if the tree were part of the house.

Bad Use of Leading Lines
Not all lines lead properly. They may lead the viewer right out of the scene.

Remedying a Tangent
An easy remedy for this example is to move the tree slightly away from the corner of the house to avoid a tangent.

With this shape, it's clear this is a dog

This shape makes it less clear what the subject is

The Shape of Your Subject Is Important
Make your drawing experience easier by looking for subjects with an outer shape that is easy to identify. The form of a dog standing is more identifiable than the form of the same dog lying down. If you were to try to draw this dog lying down, the process of sketching and shading the dog's shape could become a bit taxing.

6 Let's Draw

Be patient with yourself. Good drawing skills are developed through observation and practice. Try drawing the same demo more than once and compare your results. You will probably be surprised by the level of improvement you have made.

Each demo is done in two stages. In the first stage, you'll work through structural drawing. In the second stage you'll apply values with pencil strokes. As you work through these demos, write the date in the corner of each drawing and sign it. By doing this, you will be able to see the progression of your skills in your artwork. Save your artwork, even if you are tempted to throw it away or send it through a paper shredder. Sometimes the frustration of working on a difficult lesson overshadows the improvement that has taken place. By putting your artwork aside to view later, you allow yourself the opportunity to view it with a more objective eye, when you are more likely to appreciate the skills you have developed.

Mountain Man
Graphite on drawing paper
14" × 11" (36cm × 28cm)

Still Life

A still life with fruit is always an interesting subject for interpreting forms through shading. This is a good demo for observing the play of light and shadow on common objects.

CHECK THIS OUT

Using Basic Shapes (p. 27)   Light Effects (p. 52)
Gauging Proportions (p. 28)

Must-Have Materials

4H, HB, 4B graphite pencils • 11" × 14" (28cm × 36cm) medium-tooth drawing paper • Drawing board • Kneaded eraser

Optional, But Not to Be Overlooked

Dividers, proportional dividers or sewing gauge • Erasing shield • Pencil sharpener • Value scale (see page 50) • White vinyl eraser

1 Sketch the Bananas

Clip your paper to the drawing board. With a 4H pencil, sketch in the curved, oblong forms of the bananas. For accuracy, draw the full shape of the farthest banana, even though its image is partially blocked by the banana in the foreground.

2 Sketch the Apples

Use the 4H pencil to sketch circles for the apples. To determine the placement of the foreground circle, draw a line under the foreground banana. Line up the foreground apple with the foreground banana.

3 Define the Shapes of the Fruit

Add stems and sketch the shapes of the individual apples and bananas. You can use dividers or a gauge here to check your proportions.

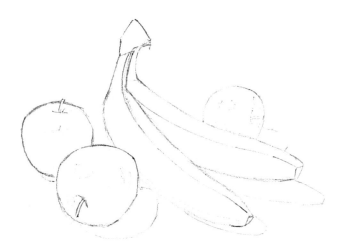

4 Add Highlights and Shadow Lines

Before using your pencil, observe the highlights and shadows. With the 4H pencil, lightly sketch where the highlights will go so you will remember to leave them white. Then sketch in where the shadows fall. Keep in mind that the primary light source is at the upper left.

5 Add Light Values to the Apples

With the 4H pencil, add value and form to the apples with light lines that follow their contours. Use uniform pencil strokes to make the surfaces look smooth.

6 Add Darker Values to the Apples and Lighter Values to the Bananas

With the HB pencil, darken the shadow areas of the apples. With the 4H pencil, indicate the lighter values of the bananas. Check your work with the value scale.

7 Add the Darker Values of the Bananas and Finish With Shadows and Background

With the HB pencil, shade the darker areas of the bananas. Use a 4B pencil to add shadows under the apples and bananas, with the darkest part closest to the fruit. Add the background value with a 4H pencil, using uniform pencil strokes. Make the apples slightly darker with a 4H pencil. Use the value scale to check your work and make any necessary adjustments. Sign and date your drawing.

Apples and Bananas
Graphite on drawing paper
11" × 14" (28cm × 36cm)

Textured Metal

For this demonstration, you want a freehand look but may need the guidance of a straightedge for steps one, two and four. Make the lines you draw with a straightedge light so they won't be so noticeable with the sketchy lines used to portray a weathered watering can.

CHECK THIS OUT

Gauging Proportions (p. 28)   Ellipses (p. 42)
Light Effects (p. 52)   Brick, Wood & Stone (p. 58)

Must-Have Materials

4H, HB, 4B graphite pencils • 11" × 14" (28cm × 36cm) medium-tooth drawing paper • Dividers, proportional dividers or sewing gauge • Drawing board • Kneaded eraser

Optional, But Not to Be Overlooked
Erasing shield • Pencil sharpener • Value scale (see page 50) • White vinyl eraser

 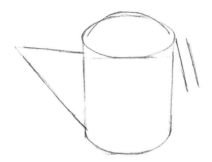 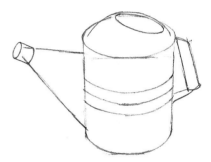

1 Draw the Cylinder of the Watering Can
With a 4H pencil, sketch a square, slightly tapered at the bottom. Draw a guideline above the square to help you place the top of the ellipse. Add height to the lines on the side, then sketch the top and bottom ellipses.

2 Add the Spout and Handle
Use the 4H pencil to sketch the lines for the spout. Use one of your proportioning tools to compare the spout width to the width of the cylinder, using this drawing as a reference. Add lines for the handle and a curved line for the top.

3 Add Details to the Watering Can
Add an angled ellipse at the top, ellipses around the central section as ribs, lines to connect the handle, and a small cylinder for the end of the spout.

4 Add Details, Including the Leaves and Boards
Add details, including the wire handle at the top and lines where the spout attaches to the body. Create the dent by changing the shape of the lines that form the ribbing. Sketch the leaf shapes around the can and vertical lines for the boards in the background. Use a kneaded eraser to remove obsolete guidelines.

5 Add Values to the Watering Can

Add lines to indicate the structure of the leaves and boards. (See page 59 for tips on drawing wood.)

With the 4H pencil, add the shading on the watering can with thin strokes going in many directions to create a weathered texture. Because the light source is at the upper left, make the left side of the can lighter than the right side.

6 Add Texture and Value to the Leaves and Boards

Shade the leaves, using an HB pencil for the soft line work and a 4H pencil for light, thin line work. With a 4H pencil, add the appearance of wood grain to the boards.

Give Your Line Work Character

Sketch over the lines you created with a straightedge to give them a more freehand look.

7 Add Darks and Details

Using 4H, HB and 4B pencils, add darks and details. Pinch the end of the kneaded eraser so it makes a point, and gently rub it on the paper to create lighter areas, such as the top of the ribs. Sign and date your artwork.

Watering Can
Graphite on drawing paper
11" × 14" (28cm × 36cm)

95

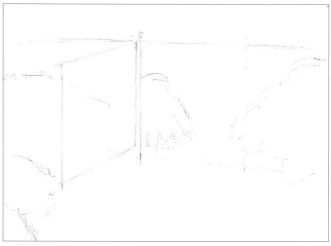

Scene in Perspective

Though it may not be obvious, this scene uses two-point perspective, so pay attention to the subtle angles of the wall and the gate. Proportion the gate correctly by using dividers, proportional dividers or a sewing gauge to compare the width of the gate's opening to the opening's height.

CHECK THIS OUT

Gauging Proportions (p. 28)   Rocks (p. 60)
Two-Point Perspective (p. 36)

Must-Have Materials

4H, HB, 4B graphite pencils • 11" × 14" (28cm × 36cm) medium-tooth drawing paper • Dividers, proportional dividers or sewing gauge • Drawing board • Kneaded eraser • Value scale (see page 50)

Optional, But Not to Be Overlooked

Erasing shield • Pencil sharpener • White vinyl eraser

1 Sketch the Basic Lines of the Walk and Gate
Start by sketching the stone walk and the opening for the gate using a 4H pencil. Use your proportioning skills and tools to make sure the proportions are correct.

2 Add the Foliage
Lightly sketch the outer shapes of the foliage with a 4H pencil.

3 Add Structural Details
Sketch the details of the gate, foliage and stones. Erase any unnecessary guidelines with a kneaded eraser.

4 Start Adding Values
With your value scale as a reference for the rest of this demo, use a 4H pencil to add values to the gate. Direct your pencil lines to follow the grain of the wood. Make the values of the shadowed side of the gate gradate from dark at the top to light toward the bottom.

5 Add Values to the Foliage
With a 4H pencil, add values to the foliage. Draw the various types of leaves differently from one another, using differing values and line strokes. Make the shadows behind the leaves darker than the leaves themselves.

6 Add Values to the Ground and Stones
Add values to the stonework and to the ground around and between the stones with a 4H pencil. (See page 58 for tips on creating the texture of stone.)

7 Finish With Details and Darks
Add the finishing details and additional darks using 4H, HB and 4B pencils. Check the range of your values with your value scale and darken areas as needed. Sign and date your drawing.

Garden Gate
Graphite on drawing paper
11" × 14" (28cm × 36cm)

Natural Textures

This fun drawing explores different textures, such as tree bark and fur. This is another drawing that could easily be made into a greeting card. It could also be framed and given to your favorite niece or nephew.

CHECK THIS OUT

Using the Basic Shapes (p. 27)   Creating Values (p. 51)
Gauging Proportions (p. 28)

Must-Have Materials
4H, HB, 4B graphite pencils • 11" × 14" (28cm × 36cm) medium-tooth drawing paper • Drawing board • Kneaded eraser

Optional, But Not to Be Overlooked
Dividers, proportional dividers or sewing gauge • Pencil sharpener • Value scale (see page 50) • White vinyl eraser

1 Sketch the Faces
Observe the basic shapes that make up the raccoons' faces before beginning. Using a 4H pencil, sketch ovals to represent the outlines of the raccoon's faces. Sketch vertical lines for the centers of their faces and horizontal lines for the placement of their eyes, which are below the middles of the ovals. Next, draw small ovals for the snouts.

2 Continue Refining the Faces and Indicate the Tree
Add shapes representing the eyes, ears and noses. Draw the hole, trunk and small oval for the paw.

3 Erase Extra Lines
Erase guidelines with a kneaded or white vinyl eraser before continuing with your drawing.

4 Add Details to the Raccoons
Add lines to indicate important details, including guidelines to indicate the markings on the raccoons' faces, the the paw and the tree bark.

5 **Begin Adding Values**
Still using a 4H pencil, begin adding the lighter values to the raccoons and the tree.

6 **Add Dark Values**
Now, using a 4B pencil, add the dark values. Keep small highlights in the eyes to suggest their glossiness.

7 **Add Middle Values and Finishing Details**
Add fur and finishing details with an HB pencil, checking the range of your values with the value scale. Lighten or darken areas as needed. Sign and date your drawing.

Little Rascals
Graphite on drawing paper
11" × 14" (28cm × 36cm)

Using Contrast

This demo shows how to rely more on value contrasts than on pencil outlines to define shapes. The light source in this scene is at the top right, but the snow also reflects light, making the wolf's outline light as well. This looks dramatic against the dark of the mountains. When collecting your supplies, include your value scale and proportioning devices so they will be handy when you need them.

CHECK THIS OUT

Using Basic Shapes (p. 27)
Gauging Proportions (p. 28)
Contrast (p. 49)

Creating Values (p. 51)
Lines, Tangents & Shapes (p. 90)

Must-Have Materials

4H, HB, 4B graphite pencils • 14" × 11" (36cm × 28cm) medium-tooth drawing paper • Copier paper to be used as a friskett • Dividers, proportional dividers or sewing gauge • Drawing board • Kneaded eraser • Value scale (see page 50) • White vinyl eraser

Optional, But Not to Be Overlooked

Erasing shield • Pencil sharpener • Scissors • Straightedge, triangle or angle ruler

1 Draw the Basic Shapes

Using a 4H pencil, sketch the basic shape of the body and the slope of the hillside. Add a circle for the basic shape of the head. While you may be tempted to rush on to the next step, this is the time to pay attention to proportions so the finished drawing will be accurate. Use a proportioning device to check your work, making adjustments as necessary.

2 Sketch the Overall Shape of the Body

With the 4H pencil, sketch the shape of the body, including the legs, neck, ear, mouth, lower jaw and tail. Pay close attention to the placement of the line for the belly because this will affect how tall the legs appear. Check your work with a proportioning device and make adjustments as needed.

3 Add Detail Lines to the Wolf and Sketch the Mountains

Erase obsolete guidelines with your white vinyl eraser and add details to the face, including the eye and nose, with the 4H pencil. Suggest the texture of the coat with back-and-forth lines along the outline of the body and within the body itself. Sketch in the mountains. Pay attention to where the lines of the wolf meet the lines of the mountains, making sure you do not create unwanted tangents (see page 90).

4 Start Adding Values

With a 4H pencil, add shading to the wolf, letting your pencil strokes follow the direction of the fur. With the exception of the head, keep the outer edges of the wolf light to suggest the light from the sky and the light reflected off the snow. This is a good place to start referring to your value scale as you lay down lights and darks for the rest of this demo.

5 **Add Darks and Details to the Wolf**
With the HB pencil, add the darker values to the coat and the shadow areas. Add facial details by darkening the eye, nose and mouth, leaving white spaces to indicate teeth. Add dots to the wolf's muzzle to suggest whiskers.

6 **Add Lighter Values to the Distant Mountains**
Using the 4H pencil, make back-and-forth strokes, filling in the mountains except for the area in direct sunlight.

7 Add the Darks of the Trees

With the HB pencil, indicate the exposed rock of the mountains with short back-and-forth strokes.

8 Add the Dark Background Trees

With a 4B pencil, use vertical pencil strokes to add the dark areas of the background trees. To do this, cut a piece of copier paper in the same curve as the hillside. Use this as a frisket to create a clean edge, as discussed on page 15.

Add Finishing Touches

9 Now to step back from your drawing to observe the range of lights and darks in the sky. Before you attempt to add the sky, consider practicing this step on a piece of scrap paper. Using a 4H pencil, add light values to the sky with long, horizontal lines. Start with light pressure at the top and gradually decrease the pressure as you work down. If you get frustrated, leave the sky white; your drawing will still be dramatic. Be encouraged. You can come back and try this again at a later date for better results. Either way, sign and date your drawing.

Call of the Wild
Graphite on drawing paper
14" × 11" (36cm × 28cm)

Expressive Portrait

Good art begins with an interesting subject. Be on the lookout for inspiring subjects because your best art will no doubt come from this inspiration. For portraits, sketch the facial structure first. Look into a mirror and use your own features as a guide. This will help you place elements such as the hat and beard with less guesswork. Apply line work in a rough and irregular manner to complement the rugged appearance of the subject.

CHECK THIS OUT

Gauging Proportions (p. 28)　　　Face: Front View (p. 82)

Human Figures (p. 78)

Must-Have Materials

4H, HB, 4B graphite pencils • 14" × 11" (36cm × 28cm) medium-tooth drawing paper • Drawing board • Kneaded eraser

Optional, But Not to Be Overlooked

Dividers, proportional dividers or sewing gauge • Pencil sharpener • Small mirror • Value scale (see page 50) • White vinyl eraser

1 Sketch the Face

With a 4H pencil, sketch the overall shape of the head and lines for the eyes and center of the face. The head is viewed slightly from the side, making the center line of the face somewhat left of center. Sketch in lines for the mouth and nose. Add the eyes.

2 Sketch Facial Features and the Top of the Hat

Sketch facial features, including the eyebrows, ears, nose, lips, pupils, irises and creases around the eyes, using the 4H pencil. Now is the time to adjust the facial features, if necessary. I decided to make the nose shorter from what I originally sketched. Add the top of the hat and band. Notice that much of its form follows the shape of the head. Add a curved line to indicate the major fold of the hat.

3 Add the Brim, Shoulders and Arms
Using the 4H pencil, add the brim. Notice the sides are turned up. Add lines to indicate the arms and shoulders.

4 Add the Hair, Beard and Details
Sketch in the basic form of the hair, beard and mustache. Add details throughout the drawing, erasing the obsolete guidelines in the process with a kneaded eraser. Make minor adjustments to the hat, if necessary.

Use a Small Mirror
Consider looking in a mirror throughout this demo to observe your own features so you will better understand the structure and values of the face.

5 **Add Values to the Face**
With the 4H pencil, add values to the face. Pay particular attention to the eyes; they are the soul of a portrait. Continue adding values to the face using the HB pencil for the darker places such as the creases near the eyes, the eyebrows and the nostrils. Leave the lightest areas on the cheeks completely white as highlights.

6 **Shade the Underside of the Hat**
Now add values to the underside of the hat brim. Use back-and-forth strokes to indicate the shape of the hat's underside. Use a 4H pencil for the light areas and an HB pencil for the dark, shadowy areas near the face.

7 Add Details to the Top Portion of the Hat

Use a 4H pencil to add values to the top part of the hat. Add fewer lines for the lighter areas. Use the HB pencil for the darker shadow areas under the band and for the very top fold of the hat.

8 Add Details to the Hair and Beard

With lots of squiggly lines, draw in the hair and beard using 4H and HB pencils. Notice that the lighter areas have fewer lines.

Mountain Man
Graphite on drawing paper
14" × 11" (36cm × 28cm)

9 Refine the Shirt and Add Finishing Details

Add the shirt and suspenders with a 4H pencil for the lighter areas, an HB pencil for the darker areas. If you feel that you drew the shoulders too low, add more to them along the top. Add additional darks and details. Sign and date your drawing.

Telling a Story Through a Drawing

This is a great demo for learning more about how to draw people. Clothing and props can tell a story to add interest to a drawing.

CHECK THIS OUT

Using a Frisket (p. 15)   Face: ¾ View (p. 83)
Gauging Proportions (p. 28)
Human Figures (p. 78)

Must-Have Materials

4H, HB, 4B graphite pencils • 14" × 11" (36cm × 28cm) medium-tooth drawing paper • Copier paper to be used as a frisket • Dividers, proportional dividers or sewing gauge • Drawing board • Kneaded eraser • Value scale (page 50)

Optional, But Not to be Overlooked

Pencil sharpener • Scissors • White vinyl eraser

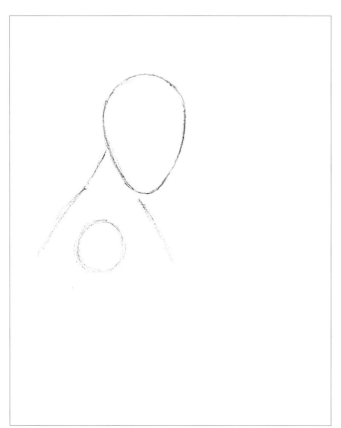

1 Draw the Basic Shapes of the Head, Neck and Shoulder

With a 4H pencil, sketch an egg-shape for the head, in three-quarters view. Sketch the neck and shoulders. Add a circle indicating the shoulder joint. Check your proportions with one of the proportioning tools.

2 Add the Arm and Hand

Add lines for the upper and lower forearm. For correct proportions, compare the length of the upper and lower arm to the height of the head, using one of the proportioning tools. Sketch lines for the hand and basket. Add lines that indicate the ridges of the hand's knuckles and thumb. At this stage, the hand should look like a mitten, since the individual fingers are not yet defined. Sketch lines to indicate the sides and bottom of the basket.

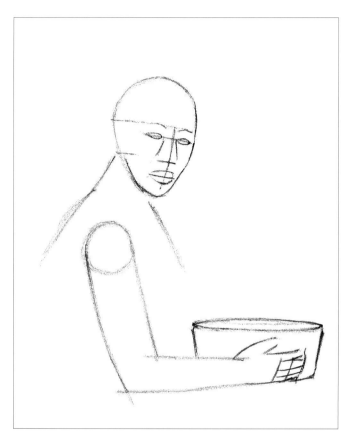

3 Sketch the Features and Fingers

Sketch in placement lines for the eyes and nose, and add a line for the center of the face. Sketch ellipses for the basket. Then go back and refine the eyes, nose, mouth and eyebrows. Add the individual fingers on the hand. To see which fingers are longer and shorter, you may want to look at your own hand and draw accordingly.

4 Continue Defining the Face, Hand and Arm and Indicate the Clothing

Sketch the ear and add more definition to the facial features, arm, hand and fingers. Erase any obsolete guidelines with a kneaded or white vinyl eraser. Add the basic form of the clothing and head scarf, noting where major folds occur. Also add short lines indicating the arm on the far side of the basket.

5 **Add Details and Begin Shading**
Sketch in the vegetables, the weave of the basket and the jewelry. Add details to the clothing, basket and ear. Erase any obsolete guidelines with a kneaded or white vinyl eraser. Add very light lines to indicate value variations on the face, neck and arm. Use the value scale to check the appropriate value changes. Keep in mind that the light source is at the upper left, so shade accordingly. Lighten some of the pencil work on the forehead, cheek, nose and arm by gently pressing a kneaded eraser on these areas to lift some of the graphite.

6 **Add Darker Values to the Face, Neck, Arms and Hands**
With an HB pencil, darken the neck, the far side of the face and under the nose and lips. Define the eyes and ear, darkening any area in shadow. Darken the arms and hand, making the farthest arm darker than the nearest arm. Use the value scale to check the values. Add a few details to the fingers, but keep the details to a minimum as the fingers are mostly in shadow.

Add the Background

7 With the HB pencil, begin adding the darks of the background. Use the value scale to create the appropriate level of lights and darks. Confine your marks to the top and left sides of the background. To make a clean edge, use copier paper as a frisket and proceed with downward pencil strokes. After you've done some of the background with the frisket, remove it and continue putting in the background without the frisket, giving the border a rough, loose look.

Darken the Background and Add Light Values to the Clothing

8 Use the HB pencil to make up-and-down strokes to further darken the values of the background. With the 4H pencil, add the lighter values to the clothing. Add interest to the composition by continuing the clothing on the left beyond where the dark of the background ends.

9 **Add Darks to the Clothing**
With an HB pencil, add the darks to the clothing. Use the value scale to help you add the appropriate values. The creases of the clothing will most likely be very dark.

10 **Add Light Values to the Basket and Vegetables**
With a 4H pencil, start adding values to the basket, keeping some areas light to show the weave. Use subtle value changes for the vegetables, with the lightest areas on the left.

11 **Add Darks to the Basket and Vegetables and Add the Finishing Details**
With the HB pencil, add darker values to the basket and vegetables. Use the value scale to see if you need to make any adjustments with the 4H and HB pencils. Make some areas, such as some of the clothing creases, even darker using a 4B pencil. Lighten any areas that are too dark by gently removing the graphite with the kneaded eraser. Sign and date your drawing.

Market Woman
Graphite on drawing paper
14" × 11" (36cm × 28cm)

Landscape Composition

To a beginner, full compositions can seem overwhelming. Just remember, most elaborate drawings are just a grouping of smaller drawings. This particular drawing is made up of three main subjects: the building, the tree left of the building and the sheep. Approach it with the idea that each is a separate drawing that contributes to the whole. Take your time, be patient with yourself and enjoy the process.

Must-Have Materials

4H, HB, 4B graphite pencils • 14" × 11" (36cm × 28cm) medium-tooth drawing paper • Drawing board • Kneaded eraser • Straightedge, triangle or angle ruler • Value scale (see page 50)

Optional, But Not to Be Overlooked
Dividers, proportional dividers or sewing gauge • Pencil sharpener • White vinyl eraser

CHECK THIS OUT

Gauging Proportions (p. 28)   Creating Values (p. 51)
Measuring Angles (p. 30)   Leafy Trees (p. 56)
Two-Point Perspective (p. 36)   Brick, Stone & Wood (p. 58)
Arches & Roofs (p. 44)

1 Draw the Basic Shapes
With a 4H pencil, lightly sketch a rectangle for the basic shape of the springhouse, then add a line for the roof's edge and another line for the front corner of the house. This may be a good time to get out your straightedge to help you draw accurate lines. Sketch the grass line, tree trunk, leaf canopy and ovals for the sheeps' bodies.

2 Add the Window, Door and Roof Lines
Using the 4H pencil and your straightedge, add the window and door to the springhouse along with angles to the roof. You may want to use an angle ruler to check your angles.

3 Add Details to the Building and Tree

With the 4H pencil, add more lines to define the springhouse, including additional overhang to the right side. Erase any unnecessary guidelines with a kneaded eraser. Sketch in more of the tree's structure, tapering the smaller branches that grow away from the trunk.

4 Add Definition to the Trees, Foliage and Sheep

With a 4H pencil, add more branches. Sketch the basic shapes of the tree's foliage and the bushes and shrubs along the house. Sketch the heads and legs of the sheep.

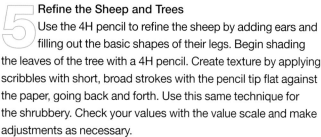

5 Refine the Sheep and Trees

Use the 4H pencil to refine the sheep by adding ears and filling out the basic shapes of their legs. Begin shading the leaves of the tree with a 4H pencil. Create texture by applying scribbles with short, broad strokes with the pencil tip flat against the paper, going back and forth. Use this same technique for the shrubbery. Check your values with the value scale and make adjustments as necessary.

6 Add Shading and Grass

Add shading to the springhouse, sheep and foliage. Use the 4H pencil for the lighter shading and the HB pencil for the darker shading. Notice that the springhouse is darker on the left side because it is in shadow.

With 4H and HB pencils, add grass to the foreground and shade the sheep further. Make the body of the sheep on the far left dark and keep the grass around it light for contrast. The bodies of the other two sheep are light, so make the grass around them darker with an HB pencil. By doing this, you won't have to rely on outlines to define the sheep; instead they are defined by contrast. Check your work with the value scale.

7 Add the Darkest Darks and Finishing Details

Make any adjustments to the shading and details with the 4H and HB pencils. Use the 4B pencil for the darkest darks, such as the window and door openings and shadow areas of the tree. Check the range of your lights and darks with your value scale and make any necessary changes. Sign and date your drawing.

Springhouse
Graphite on drawing paper
14" × 11" (36cm × 28cm)

LAUS DEO
M Willenbrink

Seascape Composition

Approach this drawing by first establishing the most difficult element to draw, the foreground boat, then work back in the distance. When shading in an area, let your line strokes follow the direction of the material you're trying to create, such as the woodgrain of the boards.

CHECK THIS OUT

Must-Have Materials

4H, HB, 4B graphite pencils • 11" × 14" (28cm × 36cm) medium-tooth drawing paper • Drawing board • Kneaded eraser • Straightedge, triangle or angle ruler

Optional, But Not to Be Overlooked

Dividers, proportional dividers or sewing gauge • Pencil sharpener • Value scale (see page 50) • White vinyl eraser

1 Sketch the Foreground Boat
With a 4H pencil, sketch the basic lines for the foreground boat. Add the curved lines of the hull and the lines of the back, or stern, of the boat. With a straightedge to guide you, sketch the side of the cabin, add the roof and the pole that supports the roof.

2 Add Details to the Boat
Add the structural features of the boat. Erase obsolete guidelines with a kneaded or white vinyl eraser. Follow this procedure to add the reflection of the boat.

3 Add the Basic Structure of the Second Boat
Sketch the second boat with the 4H pencil. This boat is viewed straight on, so the use perspective is minimal.

4 Add Details to the Second Boat
Sketch in the structure of the cabin. Add the reflection of the boat, and erase obsolete guidelines.

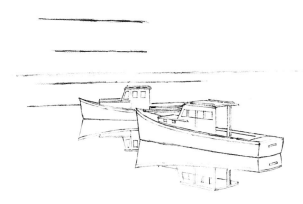

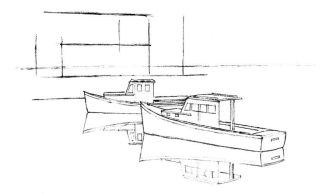

5 Sketch the Horizon and Begin the Building

You may want to use your straightedge for the following steps. Use the 4H pencil to add the horizon line, then add the horizontal lines of the building. Notice that they would converge at a vanishing point far on the distant right.

6 Add the Vertical Lines of the Building

With the 4H pencil and a straightedge, sketch the vertical lines of the building. Pay attention to their proportions and placement.

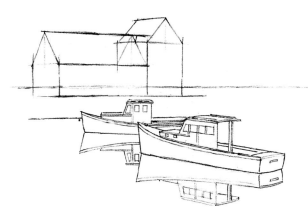

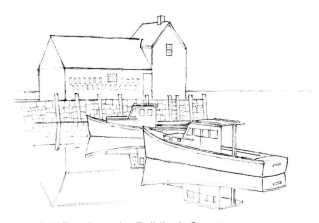

7 Form the Roofs and Gables

Add the roofs and gables with the 4H pencil and a straightedge. Some of the lines, such as the one coming from the tallest roof peak, will go toward a vanishing point on the left side.

8 Add Details to the Building's Structure

With the 4H pencil, add details to the building, including windows, door and trim and the poles and stones to the pier. You may want to check your angles with an angle ruler. Erase any obsolete guidelines.

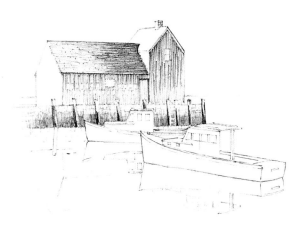

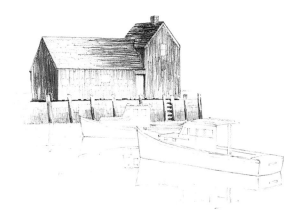

9 Start Shading the Building and Stonework

Start shading the lighter side of the building and the stonework with a 4H pencil, remembering that the light source is at the upper right. Darken the stonework near the water line. Use the value scale to check your values as you work through the rest of these steps.

10 Add the Darker Values to the Building and Stonework

Add the darker values to the roof, the chimney and the darker sides of the building with 4H and HB pencils. Use the HB pencil for the darker areas, such as adding shadows under the building.

11 Continue Adding Darks to the Building and Stonework

Continue adding more darks and details to the building and stonework with 4H and HB pencils, as necessary. Apply the darkest darks with the 4B pencil.

12 Start Adding Values to the Boats

Add the lighter values of the boats with a 4H pencil. Make the foreground boat darker than the second boat for contrast.

13 **Add Middle Values to the Boats**
Add the middle values of the boats with the HB pencil. Clean up any smudges and erase any unnecessary lines with a kneaded eraser.

14 **Add Reflections and Final Darks and Details**
Add reflections with back-and-forth horizontal strokes using a 4H pencil. Lightly indicate distant water and trees near the horizon. Add some darks to the boats with a 4B pencil and darken much of the foreground boat with the 4H pencil. Add some simple seagull shapes with a 4H pencil. Sign and date your artwork.

Rockport Harbor
Graphite on drawing paper
11" × 14" (28cm × 36cm)

Glossary

Acid-free paper. Paper that has not been processed with acid. Acid can cause paper to yellow over time.

Angle ruler. A small ruler that can fold in the middle to measure angles.

Asymmetrical. That which is not symmetrical. In reference to art, something may be balanced without being symmetrical.

Atmospheric perspective. The illusion of depth achieved through contrasts in value and definition.

Baseline. A line that establishes the placement of a subject and helps you work out the proportions of a drawing.

Blind contour sketch. A sketch or drawing done with a single line without looking at the paper.

Cast shadow. The shadow of an object that appears on a different surface or object.

Chiaroscuro. A sketch or drawing that defines the form of an object using only highly contrasting values, usually black and white, instead of with contour lines or shading.

Composition. The arrangement of elements in an artwork.

Contour sketch (or Continuous line sketch). A sketch or drawing that is done with a single line.

Contrast. Differences between the values in a composition.

Craft knife. A small knife with a sharp, pointed, replaceable blade.

Crop. Determine the area of a scene to be included within an artwork.

Dividers. A handheld compasslike device for measuring and proportioning.

Drawing. A finished representation of a subject.

Drawing board. A smooth, sturdy board placed underneath the paper for sketching or drawing.

Drawing paper. Heavyweight paper, commonly 80 lb. to 90 lb. (170gsm to 190gsm), used for drawing.

Ellipse. The shape a circle takes on when viewed at an angle. Used to show perspective.

Erasing shield. A thin metal shield used to mask areas that are not to be erased.

Eye level. *See* Vantage point.

Fixative. A spray applied to pencil drawings to prevent the artwork from smudging.

Focal point. The area or part of a painting to which the composition leads the eye, also referred to as the center of interest.

Form shadow. A shadow on an object that gives the form more dimension.

Format. The overall shape of a composition.

Frisket. A sheet of paper used as a shield to create an even edge or a clean margin beside a set of pencil lines.

Gauge. To determine specific proportions of elements in a scene.

Graphite. A soft black substance used in the core of some pencils.

Highlight. An area of light on an object, usually placed in the direct path of the light.

Horizon line. The line where land or water meets the sky, in reference to linear perspective.

Kneaded eraser. A soft, pliable gray eraser.

Lead. The term mistakenly used for graphite in a pencil. Also the scale that rates the hardness or softness of the graphite.

Leading lines. A group of compositional elements used to form lines to direct the viewer's eye to centers of interest.

Light box. A device that shines light evenly through a translucent surface. This allows the viewer to see slides, transparencies or drawings laid on its surface.

Light source. The origin of the light shining on elements in a composition.

Linear perspective. Depth implied through line and the relative size of elements in a composition.

Mechanical pencil. A pencil consisting of a thin stick of graphite encased by a holder similar to a pen. Mechanical pencils need no sharpening.

One-point perspective. A type of linear perspective with one vanishing point.

Pad. A stack of sheets of paper attached at one side with glue or wire.

Paper weight. The thickness of a sheet of paper; common weights for sketch paper are 50 lb. to 70 lb. (105gsm to 150gsm). For drawing paper common weights are 80lb to 90lb (170gsm to 190gsm).

Pencil extender. A device that attaches to the end of a pencil that has been shortened by use, used to extend the pencil's life.

Pencil sharpener. A mechanical device used to sharpen the ends of pencils.

Perspective. A technique that gives the illusion of depth to a flat picture.

Proportional dividers. Dividers that have points at both ends and are used for proportionally enlarging or reducing a hand-drawn image.

Reference materials. Pictures from various sources, used to examine a subject more closely, or from different angles, or under different conditions.

Reflected light. Light reflected off one surface onto another.

Sandpaper pad. A very small pad of sandpaper sheets attached to a handle; used for sharpening pencil tips.

Sewing gauge. A hand-held device with a moveable marking guide that can be used for measuring proportions.

Sketch. A drawing in rough, unfinished form.

Sketch paper. Lightweight paper, commonly 50 lb. to 70 lb. (105gsm to 150gsm), used for sketching.

Slip sheet. A sheet of paper placed over an unfinished drawing, under the drawing hand, to prevent the hand from smearing the graphite as it moves across the paper.

Straightedge. A metal ruler or similar tool used for drawing straight lines.

Structural sketch. The primary line work that the values (lights and darks) and line work of a drawing are built upon.

Symmetrical. Balanced composition, with equal elements placed as if reflected in a mirror.

Tangent. The unfortuante meeting of two similar compositional elements. Tangents usually detract from a composition because they can confuse the viewer.

Three-point perspective. A type of linear perspective with three vanishing points—two at the vantage point and one either above or below eye level.

Thumbnail sketch. A small, quick sketch.

Tooth. The roughness of a paper surface.

Tracing paper. Thin, translucent paper used in the process of drawing.

Triangle. A thin, transparent triangle formed out of plastic used for drawing lines.

T-square. A straightedge with a perpendicular attachment that allows the tool to glide along the side edge of a drawing board or paper pad.

Two-point perspective. A type of linear perspective with two vanishing points.

Values. Degrees of light and darkness in a sketch or drawing.

Value scale. A scale showing a range of values.

Value sketch. A thumbnail sketch used to plan the lights and darks of a drawing.

Vanishing point. A point usually on the horizon line, at which parallel lines seem to converge.

Vantage point. The point from which the viewer observes a scene.

Viewfinder. A device used to crop a scene.

White vinyl eraser. A white, squarish eraser.

Index

Watercolor for the Absolute Beginner

Bubbles
10" x 14" (25cm x 36cm)
140-lb. (300gsm) cold-press watercolor paper

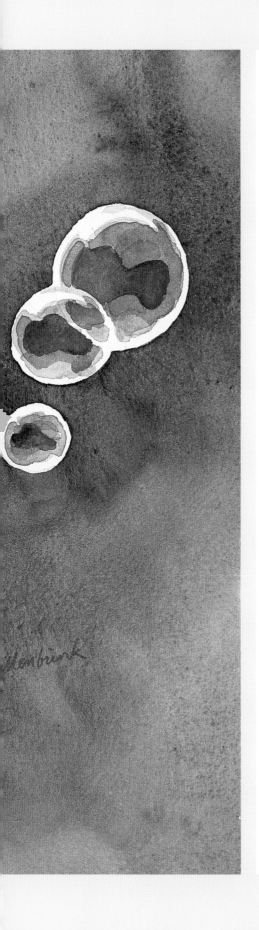

Watercolor
for the
Absolute
Beginner

Mark Willenbrink

written with

Mary Willenbrink

NORTH LIGHT BOOKS
CINCINNATI, OHIO
www.artistsnetwork.com

DEDICATION

Laus Deo

Praise to God

ACKNOWLEDGMENTS

We would like to thank those behind the scenes at F&W Publications who have made this all possible: acquisitions editor Rachel Wolf, contracts manager Julia Groh, editorial director Greg Albert, production editor Maria Tuttle, designer Angela Wilcox, production coordinator Mark Griffin and marketing director Howard Cohen. We also would like to add a special thanks to Ann, Maureen and Kelly at *Watercolor Magic* for getting us started and giving us the opportunity to try writing and illustrating as a team. We thank all of you for your time and expertise.

To Amanda Metcalf, our editor, we give our heartfelt thanks for your time, patience, listening skills and expertise. We could not have done this without you! Our relationship is blessed with confidence and peace.

We also would like to thank those who have encouraged us to take the giant step forward to write this book. To Mary's parents, Bud and Grace Patton, for your consistent encouragement to keep on writing. To Mark's parents, Roy and Clare Willenbrink, for your encouragement and support in so many ways. To Mary Helen Wallace for introducing Mark to watercolors. You and your artwork have greatly inspired me and influenced this book. Jean Bouche, thanks for the good times we had painting together and for your influence. To Dorothy Frambes for showing Mark how to apply the fundamentals of art in a practical manner while sparking his creativity. To George Soister for your friendship and expertise in photography. Tom Post, for your constant friendship, honest critiques and encouragement, which have challenged Mark to be a better artist and person. Thanks also to the talented cartoonists and illustrators at the lunch group. Being around all of you has "drawn out" the best in Mark. We would like to thank our children, family and friends who have walked through this time with us. Everyone, you've been so supportive!

Lastly, we acknowledge we could not have done this book without each other, and it is by the Lord's grace that our combined talents were able to be used not only to accomplish this book but also to grow in our marriage at the same time.

Table of Contents

Introduction

You could say that painting with watercolors is like being married. In our marriage we've found that the same things we loved about each other in the beginning drove us crazy later. As we learned more about the "art" of marriage, we learned to appreciate each other's qualities and go with the flow. Painters need to have the same relationship with watercolors. As you grow in your talents, you will be able to embrace the unique spontaneity and joy that watercolors can bring to the artist. Each painting then will become not just a product of the artist but a product of the interaction between the artist and the paint.

We hope you find a joy in watercolors with all their temperamental and lovable qualities the same way we found joy working together to create this book. We wish we could be there with you to support you and encourage you as you paint, but we're confident that you'll grow in your gifts and talents as you progress through this adventure. Just go with the flow, literally!

1

Gather the Materials

When you're prepared, sitting down to paint a watercolor is exciting. When you're not prepared, the stop-start feeling of getting up and down to find supplies or go to the store can impede your creative mood, inspiration and focus. This chapter will help you collect the right materials to prepare you for a positive experience whenever you feel inspired to paint.

Paints

I use a variety of paint brands and choose paints mostly for their color, solubility and price. Pigments of the same name can vary from one manufacturer to another. Understanding the following variables will help you determine which paints are best for you.

Grade

The biggest variable of paint is its grade. Watercolor paints are available in two grades, student and professional. Student-grade paints are less expensive, but professional-grade paints may provide more intense color and better solubility.

You may not be able to distinguish between the two at first, but after becoming more familiar with watercolors and how the paint behaves, try different colors and brands to see what appeals to you and suits your style.

Intensity

Intensity, the brightness of a color, describes the difference between brilliant and less vibrant colors.

Solubility

Solubility describes the ability of the paints to blend with water and mix with each other. The better the quality of the paint, the easier it will dissolve and the more evenly it will mix.

Lightfastness

Manufacturers often rate the degree of lightfastness, a paint's resistance to fading over time, on the package.

Packaging

I use tubes of paint instead of dry cakes or half pans. You must add water to cakes to make them workable, and the already soluble paint from a tube is easier to work with. If you'll be painting only occasionally, use 8ml or 10ml tubes. Larger volumes may be more economical, but the paint might dry out before you finish them.

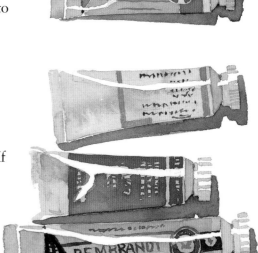

How They Differ

grade
intensity
solubility
lightfastness
packaging

student-grade   professional-grade

Different Grades
Examine the difference between these two grades of cadmium yellow. I prefer the more vibrant color of the professional-grade paint, even though it costs more than the student-grade paint. Experiment to find the paints that work best for you. You might like different colors in different grades.

Common Paints
Winsor & Newton, Cotman, Grumbacher Academy and Van Gogh student-grade paints are pictured at top. Winsor & Newton, Grumbacher, Rembrandt, Daler Rowney and Sennelier professional-grade paints are pictured above. Other brands include Da Vinci, Holbein, Schmincke, Lukas, Maimeriblue, BlockX, Old Holland, Daniel Smith and American Journey.

Palettes

Use a palette to hold and mix your paint. Your palette should have a flat, white surface with low sides. Small palettes are easier to carry, but big ones are better for mixing lots of paint. You'll also need a cover to keep dust and dirt off the palette and paints, especially when traveling. If you have an airtight cover, let your paints dry out before covering them to avoid mildew. If your cover isn't airtight, remember to carry your palette flat so wet paint won't spill. When you finish a painting, don't clean the palette and throw away good paint. Because watercolors are water soluble, you can add water and reuse them.

Plastic Plate Palette

You can transform plastic plates into inexpensive palettes. Use one plate to hold paint and the other to mix it. When you're not painting, flip one plate over the other and hold them together with binder clips. This palette is lightweight and inexpensive, so you won't have to worry about carrying heavy supplies or losing expensive ones.

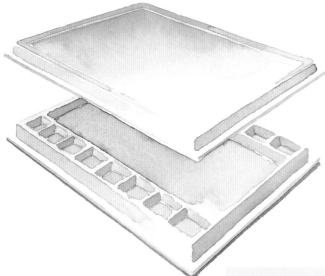

Manufactured Palettes

You can buy plastic palettes that come with paint wells and covers. Get a palette with enough wells to hold all of the colors you want (see page 11) and a surface large enough to mix lots of paint.

How They Differ

cover
shape
size

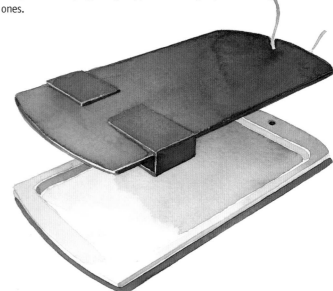

Butcher Tray Palette

A porcelain butcher tray is another option. It's sturdy, and you can place the paint anywhere you choose because there aren't any preformed paint wells. Make sure the surface of the tray is flat before you buy one; many of these trays have convex surfaces that cause paint to run together into the corners. Porcelain butcher's trays don't come with covers, so I fashioned my own with two pieces of heavy cardboard and a piece of string.

To make your own cover, cut one piece of cardboard to the same dimensions as the surface of the palette. Then wrap a strip of cardboard around the lid and palette. Attach the strip to the cardboard lid so it acts as a sleeve to slide the palette into. On the other end of the lid, make a hole and thread a shoestring through to tie the cover and palette together, or secure the lid with a rubber band.

Palette Setups

Each setup shown here progresses in complexity. Most of the colors are available in both student and professional grades. I prefer not to use white or black paint. Instead, I use the white of my paper as the white in my paintings, and I mix my rich darks from other colors. I'll talk more about color practice and theory on pages 30-33.

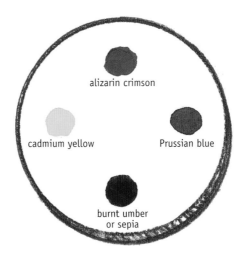

Four-Color Setup
A basic setup uses the three primary colors, red, yellow and blue, and one brown. These colors are available in student and professional grades.

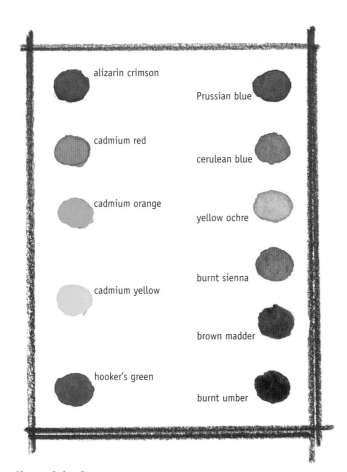

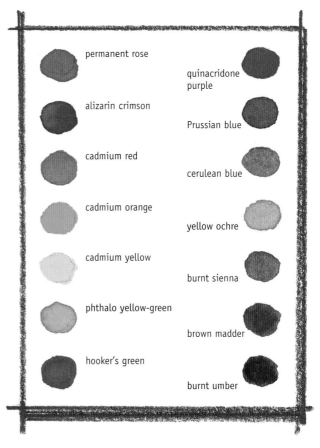

Eleven-Color Setup

This setup for the beginner provides a variety of possible combinations without using too many colors. You'll use this palette for most of the demonstrations in chapter four. All of these colors are available in both grades except for brown madder, which usually is available only in professional grade. I also recommend using professional-grade cadmium yellow.

Fourteen-Color Setup

I usually work with this setup. The additional colors are mostly available only in professional grade. Try this palette after you've gained some experience. It's fairly crowded, so sometimes I use an additional palette or the palette lid for mixing.

Paper

Your painting experience and the end result will differ based on the kind of paper you use. Some papers are harder to work with than others. Many artists use their best paper just for final paintings and other paper for sketches and practice. Consider the following variables when deciding which paper works for your style.

Quality

Student-grade paper generally absorbs paint faster and dries quicker, which makes it harder to work with than higher-grade paper. Professional-grade paper, for the most part, is better for layering and lifting paint and exhibiting the true color and brightness of paints. It's user-friendly, which makes it worth the cost.

Surface Texture

Watercolor paper's texture can be hot-press, cold-press or rough. Hot-press paper is smooth and produces hard edges and interesting watermarks when you apply paint. This kind of paper doesn't work well for gradations of color—a smooth transition from one color to another.

Cold-press paper has a moderate texture and allows smooth color gradations. Some manufacturers refer to cold-press paper, as in "not hot-press."

Rough paper is an even coarser, more textured paper. Like cold-press paper, it allows smooth color gradations, but it offers more extreme textural effects. The rough, pitted surface allows lots of the white of the paper to show through when you paint on dry paper with little water. The texture also adds interest to certain subjects, such as ocean waves.

Content

The content of the paper affects how paint responds to the paper. Most papers are made of natural substances, but some are completely synthetic or made from a combination of natural and synthetic ingredients.

As paper ages, acid can cause it to yellow. To be safe, use 100 percent cotton, acid free, pH neutral paper. Don't assume that pH neutral paper is acid free; the manufacturer may simply have neutralized the acid. Look for "acid-free." I use this paper even for practice paintings because I'm never sure when I'll want to keep one.

Tooth Translates to Texture
These color swatches show how paint looks when applied to the different kinds of paper: hot-press (1), cold-press (2) and rough (3).

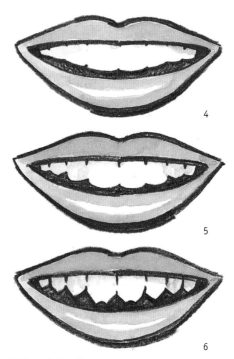

A Paper's Tooth
A paper's coarseness sometimes is referred to as tooth. Hot-press paper (4) is smooth and has very little tooth. Cold-press paper (5) has a moderate tooth. Rough paper (6) has lots of tooth.

Packaging

Watercolor paper comes in individual sheets, watercolor blocks and watercolor pads. Watercolor paper in pad form usually comes in weights of 90-lb. (190gsm) or 140-lb. (300gsm). The paper wrinkles when wet because the sheets are bound on one side only. Watercolor blocks are bound on all four sides. The individual sheets stay in place and wrinkle less. Separate each sheet after painting by running a knife around each side between the top two sheets.

Weight

The heavier the weight, the thicker the paper. Thicker paper wrinkles less after getting wet. Larger pieces of paper wrinkle more than smaller ones.

Common paper weights are 90-lb. (190gsm), 140-lb. (300gsm) and 300-lb. (640gsm). 90-lb. (190gsm) is so thin and wrinkles so easily I find it impractical. Don't use 90-lb. (190gsm) or lighter paper unless it is made from synthetic ingredients.

140-lb. (300gsm) paper can wrinkle, but it's thin enough to see through for tracing drawings and is affordable. Use this paper for any painting 12" x 16" (30cm x 41cm) or smaller.

For larger paintings, use 300-lb. (640gsm) paper. Because of the thickness of this heavy paper, even larger sheets will stay relatively flat when wet. Seeing through it to trace an image is difficult, though. It's also twice the price of 140-lb. (300gsm) paper.

For big wet-on-wet paintings, which you'll learn more about in chapter 3, you can wet both sides of a sheet of 300-lb. (640gsm) paper and then mount the paper to a board with Bulldog clips. The thick paper takes longer to dry than lower weights so you'll have more time to work on the painting before the paper starts to dry.

How They Differ

quality
surface texture
content
packaging
weight

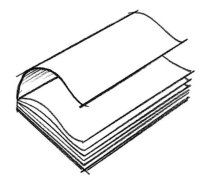

Pads
Pads are bound on one side.

Blocks

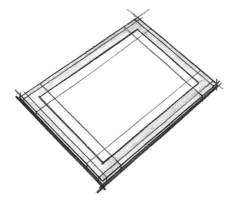

Mounting the Paper
It's economical to buy paper in large sheets, then trim them to the size you want. To prevent individual sheets of paper from wrinkling when you apply water, mount the dry paper to a thin, sturdy board, such as waterproof Masonite, plywood or watercolor board. Attach the dry paper on all four sides with 2-inch (51mm) wide sealing tape.

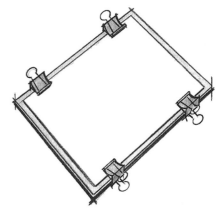

Preventing Wrinkling
You can also mount paper with binder or Bulldog clips. Though easy to use, the clips can get in the way and the paper is more apt to wrinkle than when secured with tape.

Another option is to stretch wet paper by fastening it to a sturdy board with staples or 2-inch (51mm) wide wet application tape. As the paper drys, it pulls or stretches itself into a smooth, flat sheet so the paper is less likely to wrinkle when you apply more water. Stretching may be effective, but I don't find it worth the extra effort.

Brushes

Brushes have either synthetic bristles, natural hairs or a combination of both. I can't tell much difference between them except the price; natural hair brushes cost more.

An artist's supply of brushes should include a range of shapes and sizes. Larger brushes hold more moisture and cover big areas, and smaller brushes work well for detailed work. I recommend the following collection of brushes for beginners.

Round

A good round brush has fine, stiff hairs that come to a nice, straight point and spring back to their original shape.

Bamboo

Big bamboo brushes are inexpensive and hold lots of fluid. They work well for loose, spontaneous painting in big areas, but don't expect to do detail work with them. Besides the large size, the coarse hairs don't always make a point and may seem clumsy to handle.

Flat

Flat brushes look like regular house-painting brushes with wide, flat edges. A flat brush makes wide strokes and leaves clean edges. If you find a flat brush with a round handle, you can twirl the brush as you drag it across the paper to vary the thickness of the stroke.

Hake

Hake (pronounced hockey) brushes are flat, hold lots of fluid and are relatively inexpensive. Use a hake brush for really big washes.

Care and Use

To clean a brush, just swish it back and forth in water until the paint is released from the hairs or bristles. Gently dry it on a clean rag and lay it flat. Once you're done painting, follow the instructions below. When considering quality and cost, don't underestimate the importance of owning good brushes. Cheap brushes can save money but make for a frustrating painting experience.

Storing Brushes
When you're done painting, clean your brushes and place them with the bristles or hairs up in a cup or can.

How They Differ

bristles
shape
size

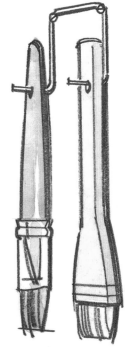

Storing Large Brushes
Drill a hole in the handles of large flat brushes, and hang them from nails, hooks or wires so the hairs or bristles hang down. If you use a nail, make sure the hole in the handle is wide enough to fit over the head of the nail. If you use a hook, make sure it's deep enough to hold the handle.

Protecting Brushes
Never stand a brush on its hairs, even in a jar of water. The hairs will bend permanently and ruin the brush's point. Also, don't squeeze the hairs to wring them dry or push down hard and scrub while painting. Brush hairs are delicate and the original shape can be bent easily. A good quality brush can last for years if you care for it properly.

Stocking Your Studio

Here's a list of everything you really need to paint in watercolors and make your way through this book. Setting aside time in your schedule to paint really helps you focus on your painting and achieve your goals. Make the most of that time by making sure you have everything you need before you start painting.

Materials List

2B pencil
2H pencil
aluminum foil
brushes
comb
cotton balls
craft knife
foam shapes (cube, sphere and cone)
graphite paper
hair dryer
kneaded eraser
masking tape
mat board
mounting board
onion bag
paints
palette
pencil sharpener
plastic wrap
Plexiglas book holder
rag
rubbing alcohol
salt
sealing tape
sewing gauge
sketch paper
sponge
spray bottle
straight edge
toothbrush
tracing paper
watercolor paper
water container
white latex house paint

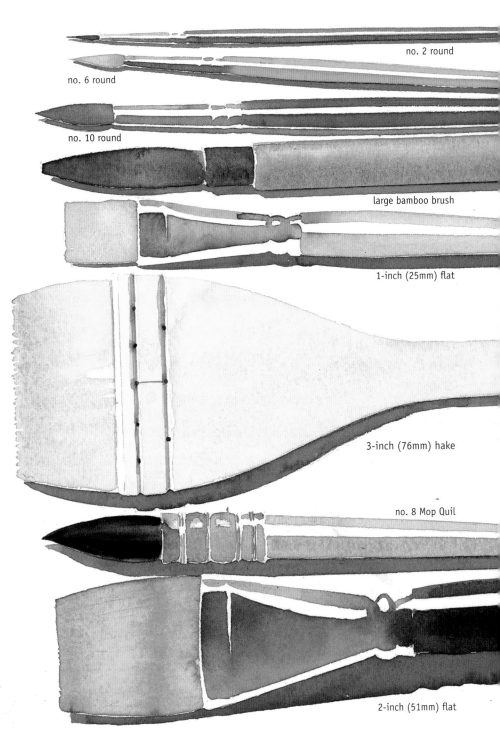

no. 2 round

no. 6 round

no. 10 round

large bamboo brush

1-inch (25mm) flat

3-inch (76mm) hake

no. 8 Mop Quil

2-inch (51mm) flat

Standard Brushes

These are all the brushes you need to paint just about anything. In addition to the types of brushes mentioned on page 14, I also like Mop Quil brushes. They combine the precise qualities of round brushes with the capacity of bamboo brushes. The hairs are not springy, but they can make a nice point. These brushes require an investment, but they're a lot of fun to paint with.

Painting in Your Studio

This is how I set up to paint in my studio. With all of these materials within reach, I'll have a productive painting session.

I cut down a gallon jug to use as a water container. It holds lots of water and has a handle and clear sides, which make it easy to see the water inside. Dry your brushes with a soft, absorbent, 100 percent cotton rag free of lint and dirt. Flannel works well. Make sure you use a light-col-ored cloth so you can tell if it's dirty. Fill a spray bottle with water for cleaning the palette and moistening your paints.

Use a 2B pencil to draw the basic forms of your composition before painting. A softer lead may smear when wetted down, and harder lead pencil is difficult to erase. Keep a pencil sharpener and a soft, gray, kneaded eraser nearby. Other erasers are abrasive and crumble too easily.

Plexiglas book holder for propping up and protecting books while painting

spray bottle

kneaded eraser

straight edge

2B pencil

pencil sharpener

water container

brushes

reference material—pictures or sketches of the subject you're painting

watercolor paper

palette

hair dryer for speeding up the drying process

rag placed within reach; I usually drape it over one knee.

Studio Setup

This is how I set up to paint. Your equipment should be within easy reach when working. It works best for me to have my tools and palette on the same side as my dominant hand and my water con-tainer just above these. I usually sit down while painting, but standing gives you freedom to move, which is especially valuable when painting big. It's important to have adequate lighting, so I make sure I have an overhead light or a desk lamp with a 100-watt bulb. Oh, and if you have a cat, it probably will claim a portion of your work surface. While you may enjoy the company, be careful because pet hair can wind up in your paints.

Painting Outdoors

You don't need an elaborate setup to paint plein air, or outdoors, so I usually pack light. You'll need paints, brushes, a palette, paper, a water container, a 2B pencil, a rag and an eraser, plus the items discussed on this page.

Plein Air Painting Supplies

You may want to bring a painting surface, such as an easel. A French easel has a drawer for storage and extra work space. Bring something to sit on, preferably something that folds up. Make sure it doesn't have arms; they get in the way when you're painting. Buy a brush holder for your smaller brushes and find a way to secure your bigger brushes to protect them. I like to carry a pair of binoculars to get a better look at things in the distance. Many artists carry cameras and sketchbooks so they can take pictures and do quick pencil studies to use as reference later.

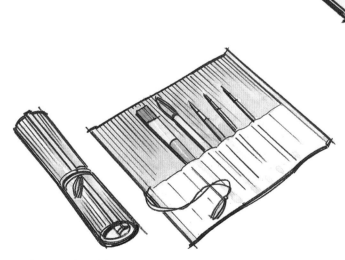

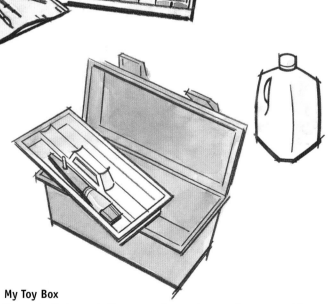

Bamboo Brush Holder

Travel can damage the bristles of smaller brushes easily. A bamboo brush holder protects brushes by keeping their hairs straight and allowing wet brushes to dry on the go.

My Toy Box

I use a tackle box as both a seat and a carrying case for my materials. Besides your regular water container, use a separate container with a lid to transport water. I protect my larger brushes by attaching them securely to the tray in my tackle box. First drill a hole in the bottom of the tray. Then run a bolt up through the hole and attach the brush with a nut. You also could attach the brush with a wire or make a cardboard sleeve.

Discussing Materials

Hot-Press Paper

What makes hot-press watercolor paper so much fun for me is the unique
watermarks that result when the paint interacts with the smooth surface.
This quality may make the paper a bit harder to work with, but as you gain
experience, you'll be able to predict these effects and feel more in control.
Then they can add so much to your artwork. To keep the feel of this painting loose, I used a large round brush as much as possible. I especially like
the effect of the watermarks on the front of the car, blending the fenders
and tires together.

Cobra
6¼" x 9" (16cm x 23cm)
140-lb. (300gsm) hot-press watercolor paper

Yupo

Unlike other kinds of watercolor paper, Yupo synthetic paper is basically a really smooth sheet of plastic. The nonabsorbent paper does not wrinkle at all and makes for a very loose painting style with hard paint edges. Because Yupo doesn't absorb paint, you can lift and manipulate color much more easily than on regular watercolor paper. You'll also need to use a large round brush that holds a lot of paint because the paint will want to come back up with the brush rather than lay on the paper. You may need to scrub the surface before you begin to get rid of grease or fingerprints, which can repel paint. Unless the surface is perfectly clean, paint won't adhere to it. Notice how the oil from one of my fingerprints seems to repel paint from the top of the post on the left.

Flower Cart
5" x 7" (13cm x 18cm)
74-lb. (160gsm) Yupo synthetic watercolor paper

Cold-Press Paper

I use Strathmore Aquarius watercolor paper at times when I want a smoother, cold-press paper. It's less prone to wrinkling than other cold-press papers because it's made from a blend of cotton and synthetic fibers. At 80-lb. (170gsm), it's thinner than most watercolor papers I use and easier to see through for tracing. Because the surface is not as soft as others, paint often doesn't seem as lively and removing pencil lines can be difficult.

Sunbathers
6" x 8" (15cm x 20cm)
80-lb. (170gsm) cold-press watercolor paper

Learn the Basics

Get back to the basics! Structure. Value. Color. An understanding of all of these components will help you create better compositions and successful paintings.

Structural Drawing

To create a successful painting, you need a solid foundation. Create an accurate drawing of the shapes and elements in a scene before you begin to paint. Structural drawing may seem too scientific or monotonous, but it's essential to the beauty of art. Structural drawings include basic shapes without shading and provide the right starting point for every painting. The basic principles of drawing follow. You may think you can't draw, but everyone can learn.

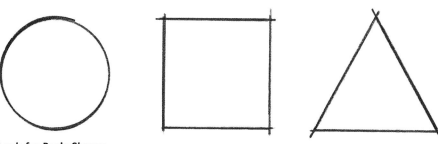

Look for Basic Shapes
Look for basic shapes such as circles, squares, triangles, ovals and rectangles.

Draw Basic Shapes
Put the big, basic shapes together.

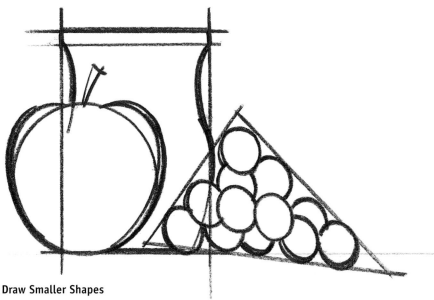

Draw Smaller Shapes
Then draw the smaller shapes, arranging them around the bigger ones. Really observe what you see. Do objects overlap? Your brain tells you an object is round, but does it really look oval? You don't have to draw tons of detail now. Leave the details for the painting process.

Measuring

Making art is a creative process, but that doesn't mean you should ignore the facts. To draw an accurate, believable object or scene, measure to get the proportions right. You can use something as simple as a pencil to measure, compare and align elements.

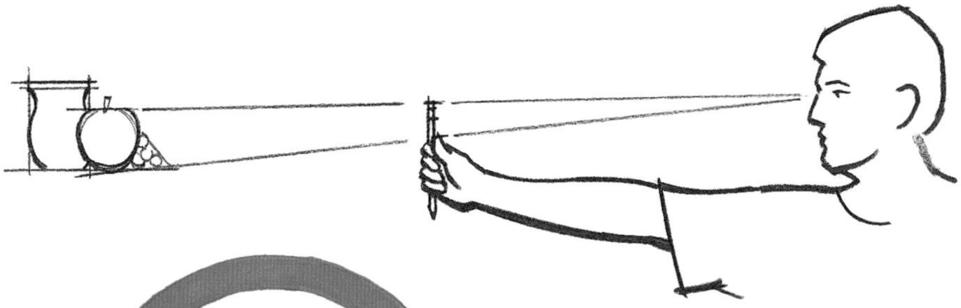

Keep It Straight

Lock your arm in a straight position, holding the pencil straight, and look at the pencil and the object you're measuring through one eye. Don't bend your arm. You'll end up with inaccurate measurements because you might bend your arm a bit differently each time. By measuring with a straight arm, your scale stays consistent from one measurement to the next.

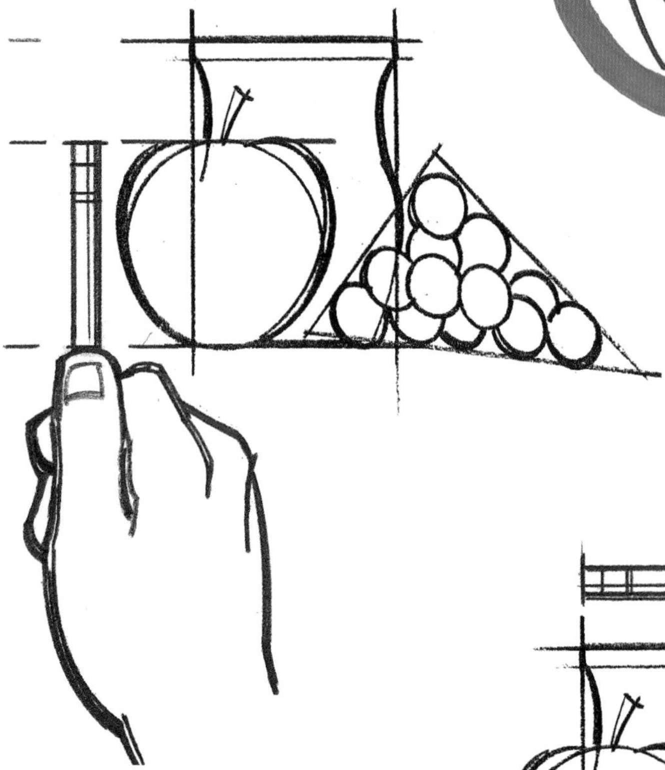

Measure Image Along Pencil

In this scene, the height of the apple equals the distance between the top of the pencil and the tip of the thumb.

Compare Measurements

Compare the measurement of the height of the apple to the width of the top of the vase. They're about the same. Comparisons like this help produce accurate drawings, especially when objects are arranged at angles.

Getting the Proportions Right
Capturing the correct proportions in a painting is the first step in achieving a realistic drawing. The building's width is twice that of the height.

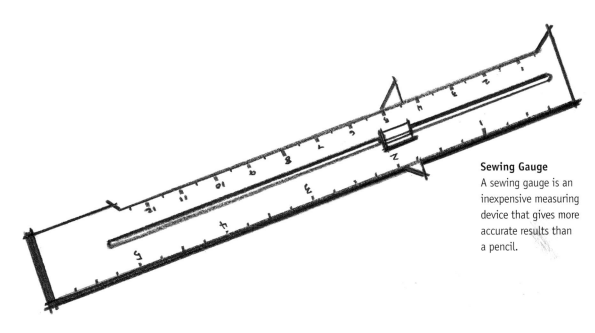

Sewing Gauge
A sewing gauge is an inexpensive measuring device that gives more accurate results than a pencil.

Drawing Linear Perspective

Perspective gives an impression of depth. When viewing an image on a two-dimensional surface, perspective makes the image look three-dimensional. Linear perspective uses lines and varies the relative sizes of objects to create this illusion.

The secret to perspective is finding the horizon. Land and sky meet on a horizon line. Somewhere on this line is at least one vanishing point where parallel lines, such as the rails of a railroad track seem to converge.

One-Point Perspective

One-point perspective is the simplest form of linear perspective, with only one vanishing point. Use one-point perspective when you're looking at an object head on.

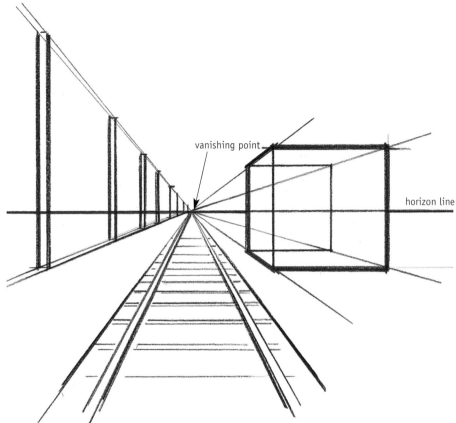

vanishing point

horizon line

Translating From a Three-Dimensional Scene to Two-Dimensional Paper
Observe one-point perspective while looking straight down a set of railroad tracks. Just make sure there's not a train in the way! The parallel tracks converge in the distance at the vanishing point. If a building or other structure is parallel to the tracks in reality, it will share a vanishing point with the tracks. If you extend the structure's line to the horizon, it will meet the others at the vanishing point rather than actually running parallel on the paper. Notice that objects of equal size in reality appear larger the closer they are to the viewer. Drawing things in perspective means drawing them not as they are in reality, but as they look from a certain viewpoint.

Two-Point Perspective

Let's look at the same railroad tracks from the side to get a glimpse of two-point perspective.

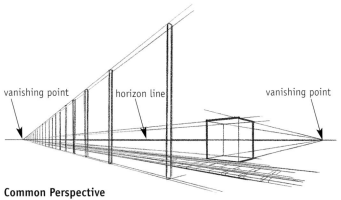

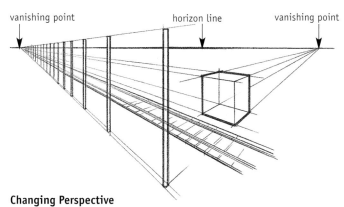

Common Perspective

The most common form of linear perspective is two-point perspective, in which two vanishing points land on the horizon.

Changing Perspective

By raising the horizon on this two-point perspective scene, the viewer now seems to be looking down on the same scene.

Hidden Vanishing Point

This scene may look simple, but planning ahead and getting factors like perspective right make the scene look accurate and believable. Even though you can't actually see the horizon in this cityscape, you should determine it's location and figure out where your vanishing point will be. Notice that all of the lines—the road, the windows and even the roofs—disappear at the vanishing point.

Understanding Value

Values are the light and dark areas of a scene. Use shading, shadows and contrasting values to provide form and definition for objects and the entire painting.

Shading and Shadows

Observe values on basic shapes to get a better understanding of shading and shadows. Use white foam shapes from your local craft store as models to examine the characteristics of light. You may need to paint the foam a light color to get an opaque surface that reflects light smoothly and accurately.

Pay attention to the direction of the light source—whether it shines from the left or right, above or below, in front of or behind the object. Once you've determined the light source, observe the lightest and darkest areas and the effect of the light source on the object's shadow.

Light

Especially when painting with watercolors, keep the light areas, as well as the shadows in mind. You can always make areas darker with watercolors, but you have to plan the light areas from the very beginning.

Contrast

Contrast is the range of dark and light between values. Value enhances the depth and clarity of a picture. Objects with values that contrast very little appear to be close together. Objects with highly contrasting values appear far apart and more defined. Look at the example right.

The darker the darks in your painting, the lighter the lights will appear. So if you want a light area to look really bright, make the objects around it dark.

Don't Be Afraid of Contrast
A picture with a low contrast of values (top) may look flat and undefined, as on an overcast day. Beginners tend to be timid with their paints, so they often end up with low-contrast paintings. A picture with a high contrast of values (above) shows depth and definition, as on a sunny day.

A Range of Values
Values don't just come in white, black and gray. Value also defines the light and dark aspects of color. For instance, the color green may appear as a light value or dark value, each portraying very different moods. In this example, the light source is located to the left and in front of the three objects.

Making a Value Scale

When you've completed this value scale, you'll be able to look through the punched holes to identify the values in a scene and determine the values you'll need for a drawing or painting. You'll need 140-lb. (300gsm) cold-press paper, burnt umber or another dark, neutral color, a no. 10 round brush and water.

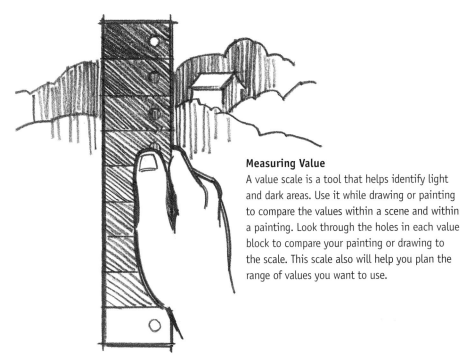

Measuring Value

A value scale is a tool that helps identify light and dark areas. Use it while drawing or painting to compare the values within a scene and within a painting. Look through the holes in each value block to compare your painting or drawing to the scale. This scale also will help you plan the range of values you want to use.

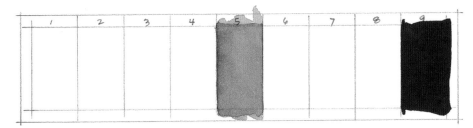

Establish Darkest and Middle Values

Divide a 10-inch (25cm) rectangular piece of 140-lb. (300gsm) cold-press paper into nine equal rectangles, leaving about a ¼-inch (6mm) border around the edges of the paper. Number the rectangles one through nine from left to right on the top border. Paint the ninth rectangle as dark as possible. Then paint in the fifth rectangle with a value about midway between the ninth value and white.

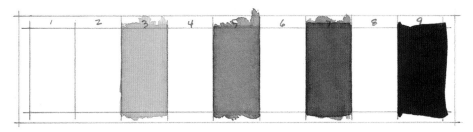

Paint Intermediate Values

Paint the third rectangle with a value between the fifth value and white. Then paint the seventh rectangle with a value between the fifth and ninth values.

Fill In Values

Paint the even numbered rectangles to make a continuous line of values that gradate from light to dark. Leave the first rectangle white. Trim all four sides and punch holes in each of the rectangles.

Understanding Color Intensity

Think of intensity as the richness or potency of a color—how yellow is a yellow, how blue is a blue—and value as the lightness or darkness of a particular color.

Some colors, such as yellow, can vary in intensity but not much in value. Other colors, such as blue, can vary in both intensity and color.

You can't control intensity like you can control value. Certain colors and paints simply have certain intensities. As you paint more often and experiment with different paints, you'll find the brands and grades of paint that suit your style.

Varying Intensities
The yellow (1) is very intense. The yellow (2) is not intense. Both are light in value. The blue (3) is very intense and has a dark value. The blue (4) is not intense with a light value.

Using Intense Colors
Both paintings use light values of yellow around the sun, but the less intense colors in the scene on the left lose the penetrating effects of the intense colors in the scene on the right.

Painting Atmospheric Perspective

Atmospheric perspective, also referred to as aerial perspective, is the use of color and value to express depth. Objects close to the viewer—in the foreground—have well-defined shapes, contrasting values and intense colors. Objects in the distance aren't as clearly defined and have more neutral values and dull, blue-gray colors.

Atmospheric Perspective
The trees show depth with atmospheric perspective but without linear perspective. Only value and color indicate depth. The darkest, most intense tree appears closest to the foreground.

Linear Perspective
The trees show depth with linear perspective but without atmospheric perspective. Size and overlapping objects indicate depth.

Combining Both Forms of Perspective
These trees show depth through both principles, creating the most realistic and appealing scene.

Understanding Color

Color, also referred to as hue, is based on the three primary colors. From these all other colors are derived.

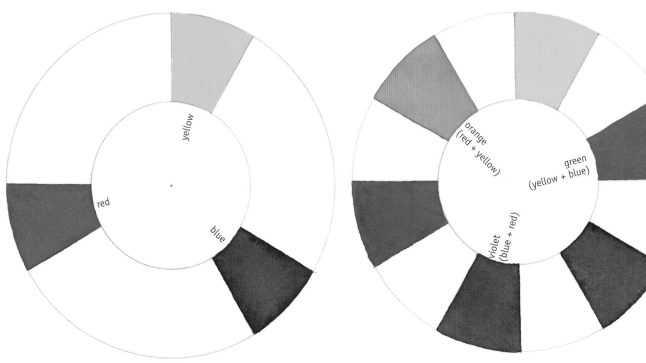

Primary Colors
Red, yellow and blue can't be made from other colors.

Secondary Colors
Orange, green and violet result from mixing two of the three primary colors.

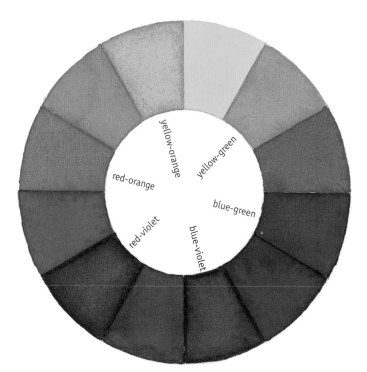

Tertiary Colors
These colors result from mixing a primary color with its adjacent secondary color.

Using Complementary and Analogous Colors

Complementary colors are any two colors that appear opposite each other on the color wheel. Analogous colors are a range of neighboring colors that make up a portion of the color wheel—red-orange, orange, yellow-orange and yellow, for example.

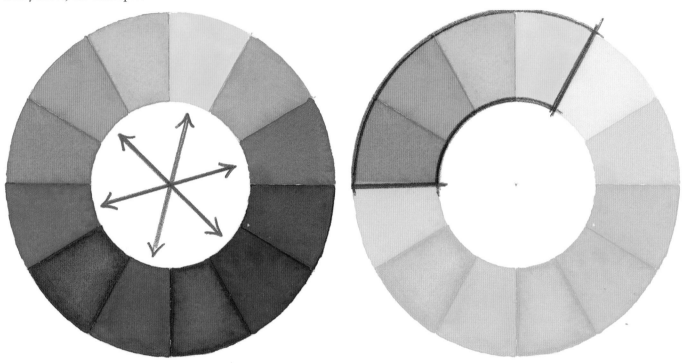

Complementary Colors
Colors that are directly opposite each other are considered a pair of complementary colors—red and green, for example.

Analogous Colors
A group of analogous colors always includes just one primary color.

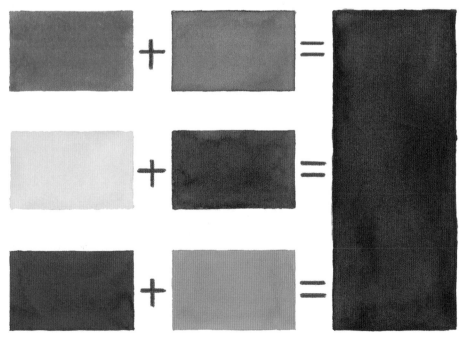

Mixing Complementary Colors
A pair of complementary colors is made up of one primary and one secondary color. If you mix a pair of complementary colors together, you've combined all three primary colors, which will result in a neutral gray or brown. If you mix the primary color red with its complement green (yellow plus blue), you'll get a brown mixture. The same result occurs if you mix yellow with its complement, violet (blue plus red), or if you mix blue and the color orange (yellow plus red).

Understanding Color Temperature

Warm colors are the reds, oranges and yellows and are also referred to as aggressive colors because they give the impression of coming forward. Cool colors, greens, blues and violets, are referred to as recessive colors because they give the impression of dropping back.

warm colors

cool colors

Assigning Temperature on the Color Wheel
Yellow-green and red-violet fall between warm and cool and can be used as warm or cool. You can use color temperature along with linear and atmospheric perspectives to emphasize depth.

Assigning Temperature to a Scene
When I'm working on a painting, I often think of the areas bathed in sunlight as predominantly warm colors and the areas in shadow as predominately cool colors.

Asymmetrical vs. Symmetrical

A symmetrical composition like the one at the right may look orderly and structured, static and bland. Let's face it: Structure can be boring sometimes, and viewers of your artwork may start to yawn. The asymmetrical composition above gives an interesting, random feel to the painting.

An Odd Way of Looking at Things

The concept of odd numbers works in more ways than one. Don't just use odd numbers of elements; also divide the painting into an odd number of parts. Imagine a grid that splits your painting into thirds horizontally and vertically. Place objects close to the intersection points of these lines to make an appealing composition.

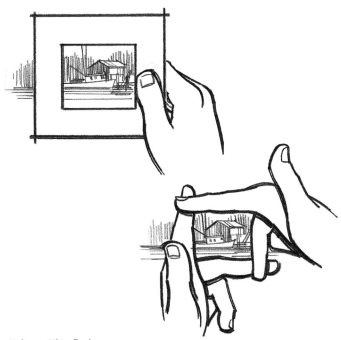

Using a Viewfinder

Some subject matter can be daunting. Landscapes in particular can be overwhelming to a painter trying to capture the great outdoors within the dimensions of a piece of paper. Use a viewfinder to focus in on a manageable composition. You can make your own viewfinder by using a craft knife and straight edge to cut a hole out of a piece of cardboard. You can also form your fingers into the shape of a rectangle.

Horizontal or Vertical

Different formats affect viewers differently. Horizontal formats lend themselves to calm, peaceful scenes. In the example above, the width of the horizontal format emphasizes the sturdiness and stability of the mountain. Vertical formats lend themselves to dramatic, intense scenes. In the example at right, the vertical format emphasizes the height and power of the mountain and gives the viewer a feeling of awe.

Don't Fence Me Out!

Walls and fences in the lower portion of a painting give an unfriendly feeling that shuts out the viewer. If you want to place a wall or fence in the foreground, add an open gate to make the scene more inviting.

Angles Add Action

Angled lines and elements give the impression of movement, which adds action and liveliness to a picture.

Plan Leading Lines

You can form lines in a composition that direct the viewer's eye to points of interest or guide the eye through the painting. In this case, the shadowy area in the foreground leads the viewer's eye to the point of interest, the deer.

Avoid tangents

Avoid Tangents

In the painting above, the handrail and two of the posts all meet at one point, called a tangent. The composition becomes confusing when the viewer can't see where one object stops and another starts. The painting at right is much easier to comprehend. It uses the same composition viewed from a different perspective.

Following the Painting Process

Watercolors are said to be unforgiving because once you've applied them to paper, they're difficult or even impossible to change. Artists can easily become overly cautious and timid with their paints, which results in a pale, stiff and unexciting painting. Instead, embrace the unpredictability of watercolors and incorporate it into your painting.

Planning

There's more to the painting process than simply applying paint to paper. To maintain control over your painting, plan ahead and to give yourself confidence. If you plan your painting well, you won't need to worry about the fact that there are no "do-overs" in watercolor. Decide on the structure, values and colors you'll use before you start painting.

Thumbnail Value Sketches
Draw a few thumbnail sketches of the scene you're going to paint on sketch paper with a 2B pencil. These small, quick sketches show different approaches to value, composition and cropping. I prefer my first sketch because the composition and values lead the eye to the focal point while producing a balanced and interesting scene.

Color Sketches
Now work up some different color schemes using the thumbnail value sketch you chose. On scrap watercolor paper, draw the structural lines without the values. Then try different color schemes, paying attention to the values of the colors you're auditioning. I prefer the direction and balance created by the use of warm and cool colors in my second color sketch. I'll use this as a reference for my final painting.

Drawing

Once you're satisfied with your composition, values and colors, draw the structural drawing that will serve as the basis of your final painting. If you're confident in your drawing skills, go ahead and draw directly onto your watercolor painting. Be careful, though. If you redraw or erase too much before painting, you'll damage the paper so paint will streak and spot. If you prefer, take a few extra minutes to draw the structural drawing on a regular sheet of paper and then trace or transfer it to watercolor paper once you're satisfied with it.

Tracing

To trace your structural drawing, you'll need a form of backlighting. Secure a piece of watercolor paper over the structural drawing with masking tape. Then attach both to your light source: a light box or a window. Trace the image with a 2B pencil. If you need to erase any lines, use a kneaded eraser, which is less abrasive than other erasers.

Heavy watercolor paper, such as 300-lb. (640gsm) paper, is too thick to use for tracing. Watercolor paper in block form is also impractical for tracing. If you're using thick paper or a watercolor block, you can transfer the structural drawing onto your watercolor paper (see page 40) rather than trace it.

Structural Lines
With a 2B pencil, lightly draw the structure of the subject onto watercolor paper. Don't worry about indicating values here; just draw the structural lines.

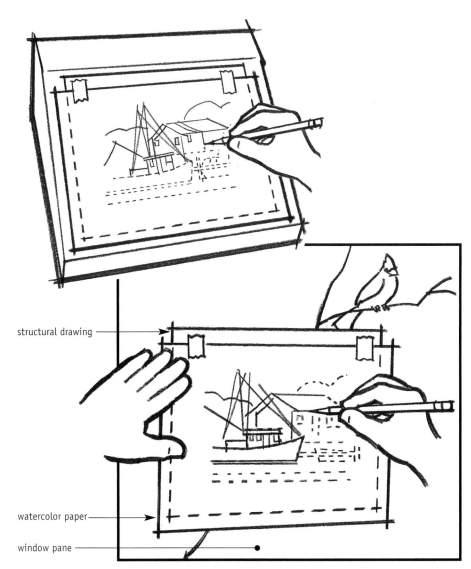

structural drawing

watercolor paper

window pane

Light Sources for Tracing
You can use a light box or a window as backlighting when tracing an image onto watercolor paper. The light outside must be brighter than the light inside so you can see through the watercolor paper. Try to find a window where you can sit to trace.

Transferring

To transfer an image, you'll need a graphite transfer sheet. As you press down on the transfer sheet, graphite transfers onto the watercolor paper. I make my own transfer sheets because commercial versions leave waxy lines that repel paint from the watercolor paper and are hard to erase.

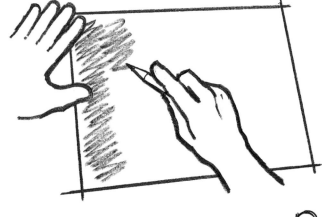

Make Graphite Paper
Cover one side of an 11" x 14" (28cm x 36cm) piece of tracing paper with graphite using a 2B pencil. Zigzag down the paper in columns until the paper is completely and evenly covered. Rotate your paper forty-five degrees and repeat this process so the new lines crisscross the original ones.

Bind Graphite to Paper
Dampen a cotton ball with rubbing alcohol and wipe it across the graphite. The rubbing alcohol evens out the graphite and binds it to the surface of the paper so it's no longer powdery. Keep the surface as dry as possible while smearing the graphite, to avoid wrinkling the paper. Some wrinkling is bound to happen, but too much alcohol—and it doesn't take much—will keep the paper from lying flat. Let the sheet dry.

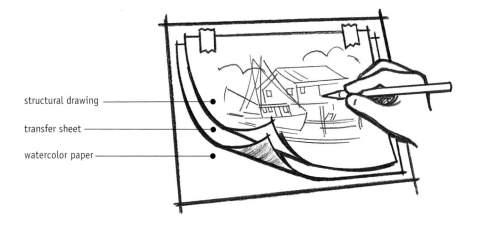

structural drawing

transfer sheet

watercolor paper

Transfer Image
With the graphite side facing down, place the transfer sheet on top of the watercolor paper and then place the structural drawing face up on top of the transfer sheet. Tape the sheets together with masking tape so they won't slip. Then go over the lines of the structural drawing with a hard lead pencil, such as a 2H pencil, and press hard enough to transfer the image, but not so hard as to leave deep grooves in the water-color paper. Check to make sure the image is transferring to your watercolor paper before you get too far into the process.

Painting

Now you've got a structural drawing on your watercolor paper whether from a direct drawing, tracing or transferring. If the paper you're working on is in block form, you're finally ready to start painting. If you're working on a loose sheet of watercolor paper, mount it to a board or stretch it with sealing tape or clips as described on page 13, then start painting.

Time to Paint
Once the paint is dry, erase your pencil lines with a kneaded eraser, sign and date your painting and you're done!

Miss Edna, Mooring
5½" x 8" (14cm x 20cm)
140-lb. (300gsm) cold-press watercolor paper

Discussing Basic Principles

Linear Perspective

Linear perspective brings realism and believability to a painting, especially architectural subjects. As I drew this building, I established the two vanishing points, using a straight edge for accuracy. I established atmospheric perspective, too, using brown madder, a warm color in the foreground and the cooler Prussian blue in the sky and background. I mixed the two colors for the cool, dark shadows. Notice that the lightest part of the building is closest to the viewer. I painted this scene from a reference photo taken on a sunny Sunday morning when the contrast between light and dark areas was strong. The building itself isn't the most likely subject, other factors like the perspective and composition of the scene made it an interesting and fun picture to paint.

WW Market
9½" x 7½" (24cm x 19cm)
140-lb. (300gsm) hot-press watercolor paper

Atmospheric Perspective

Using atmospheric perspective in addition to linear perspective adds a feeling of depth to scenes like this painting. I took one of my classes to this location for a plein air painting demonstration. Painting plein air forces you to work quickly while really observing the subject. The class studied the way the sky and shadows looked when we started painting, and made a mental note to follow that guide. The light source, the sun, in plein air painting is constantly changing, so you have to keep it consistent in your painting even if it is changing in reality. Notice that the colors in the foreground in this painting are richer and more intense with more contrast, while the background colors are cooler and more muted and neutral. When painting plein air, you can work on a painting or just a sketch that you'll use to paint a final painting later. Either way, the important thing is to relax and enjoy the experience. Whether you end up with a masterpiece or not, you'll improve your observation and technical skills, which are invaluable to future paintings.

Meadow Trail
12" x 16" (30cm x 41cm)
140-lb. (300gsm) cold-press watercolor paper

1
2
3
4

Practice the Techniques

Painting with watercolors is fun, and it's even more exciting when you learn the techniques unique to this particular medium. In this chapter you'll learn some easy techniques that will bring more creativity, interest and enjoyment to your watercolor painting experiences.

Mixing Paint and Handling Brushes

Unlike other mediums, watercolor paints are supposed to be used transparently to utilize their luminescent qualities, so you have to mix the paint with water before applying it to paper. Whenever I talk about a color in this book, I'm referring to a mixture of water and paint. The ratio of paint to water that you should use depends on how light or dark you want a color to be. Only hands-on experience can teach you how much water and paint to use to get the results you want.

The idea behind mixing colors is to start with a base color, or the lightest color, and then add small amounts of the darker color or colors until you get the color you want. If two colors are equally dark, think back to the color wheel. Green and blue can be equally dark, but green is made up of yellow and blue. Yellow is lighter than blue, and green has yellow in it, so it should be the base color. Start with green and add bits of blue until you get the color you want. Then add water until you get a good, working consistency.

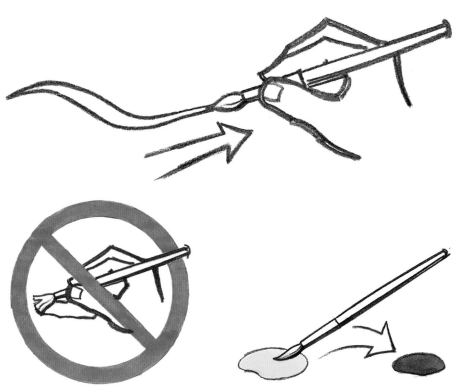

Using Brushes Correctly
Watercolor brushes can be pricey. Handle them carefully to get the most mileage out of them. A good round brush has bristles that come to a fine point. To maintain the point, gently pull or draw the brush away from the hairs toward the handle as you paint. Pushing or scrubbing with a brush can ruin the fine point that your brush once made.

Mixing Colors
Start with the lighter colors. Darker colors are more dominant than lighter colors and can overpower them.

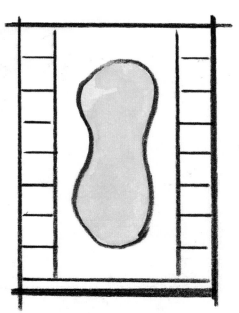

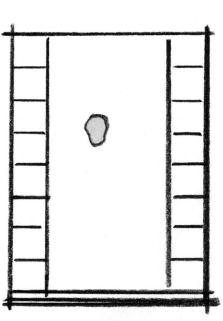

Don't Skimp
Don't worry about using too much paint or water. Beginners often mix too little and then try to stretch what little they have. This means your paint application will be weak and pale or you'll spend lots of time trying to make another mixture of the exact same color and value to finish your painting. The mixture at left is much more realistic than the mixture at right. "Fresh squeezed" paints from the tube are more soluble than paints that have dried out on your palette. Use fresh paints to avoid pale colors.

Painting Wet-on-Wet

To work wet-on-wet, apply a brush loaded with paint to wet paper. This technique offers less control than wet-on-dry or dry-brush techniques, which you'll learn about on page 48, but it also offers plenty of unique and unexpected results. Applying paint wet-on-wet allows the painter to use loose strokes and bold colors.

Time is of the essence when you're working wet-on-wet because you need to finish painting the area before the paper dries. Choose your colors and mix lots of paint and water on the palette before you wet the paper. Use a big, wide brush to cover the area with water just before you begin to paint so the whole area is covered with a smooth, even sheen. If the paper is too wet or too dry, the color won't bleed out smoothly.

The paint should transfer easily from the brush to the paper and spread to areas where the paper is wet.

Apply Water
Wet the surface of the paper with a wide, flat brush filled with water. Use long, straight, back-and-forth strokes. The entire area you want to paint should have an even sheen just before you start painting.

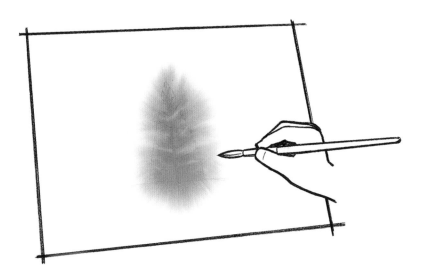

Apply Color
Load a brush with paint and gently touch or sweep the brush along the paper surface so the color transfers from the brush to the damp paper. Remember that these are watercolors—trying to brush the paint into submission once it's been applied can cause smearing. After the color leaves your brush, let the spontaneity of watercolors take over.

What Paper to Use

The smooth surface of hot-press paper doesn't allow paint to spread out as much as cold-press or rough paper does, though I do like the interesting watermarks and hard edges. If you want to create soft edges with the wet-on-wet technique, use cold-press or rough paper.

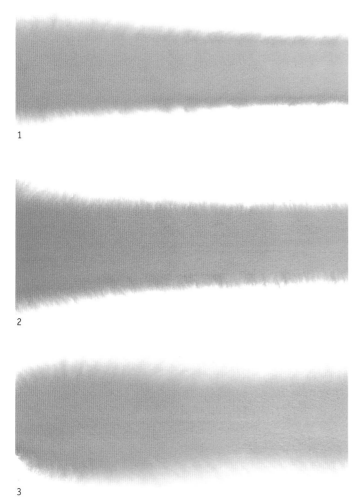

1

2

3

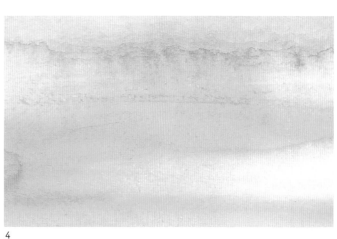

4

5

Wet-on-Wet on Different Papers
Examples of this painting technique on different papers appear above: hot-press (1), cold-press (2) and rough (3).

How Much Water Do I Use?
The trick when painting wet-on-wet is to apply just the right amount of water to the paper before painting. If the surface is too wet (4), it won't want to accept the color, and you'll get pale, uneven results. Before adding color, gently smooth any puddles of water so you have a thin, even sheen of water over the paper's surface. If the surface is too dry (5), the color may bleed out in an inconsistent manner. Don't get frustrated. It may take some practice to learn how much water to use.

Painting Wet-on-Dry and Drybrushing

Wet-on-wet, wet-on-dry and dry-brush techniques are synonymous with watercolor. Often, all three are used in one painting.

Wet-on-Dry

To paint wet-on-dry, apply a wet brush loaded with paint to dry paper. Because there is no water on the paper to help the paint disperse, wet on dry produces defined strokes with hard edges. Different papers react similarly to the wet-on-dry technique. However, the smooth surface of hot-press paper allows cleaner edges.

Dry Brush

The dry-brush technique uses dry paper and a dry brush loaded with a mixture that has very little water. Hot-press paper lets very little texture show through after you've painted over it. Rough paper shows plenty of texture. If you want to use wet-on-dry or dry brush techniques, make sure the area is completely dry before painting.

Wet-on-Dry on Different Papers
Examples of this technique used on different papers appear above: hot-press (1), cold-press (2) and rough (3).

Dry Brush on Different Papers
Examples of this technique used on different papers appear above: hot-press (4), cold-press (5) and rough (6).

Use Very Little Water for Drybrushing
Mix the paint with just enough water to allow the mixture to transfer from the brush to the dry paper. The example far left shows too much water used.

Applying a Flat Wash

A flat wash covers a large area with even color. You need to work quickly to cover the surface evenly, finishing the wash before any part dries.

Make a generous mixture on your palette so you'll have enough paint to work quickly. For big washes, use a second palette or the palette cover so you'll have enough room to create a big mixture.

Paper quality makes a big difference when painting washes. In general, professional-grade paper stays wet longer, providing more time to work on the wash. Good paper also accepts multiple washes better than student-grade paper. For paintings larger than 11" x 17" (28cm x 43cm), use nothing thinner than 300-lb. (640gsm) paper to prevent wrinkling.

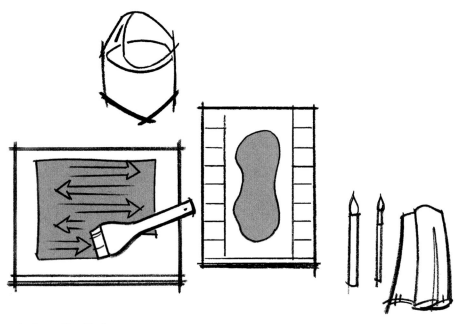

Flat, Even Color
A flat wash covers the paper evenly and doesn't vary in value or color.

Painting a Flat Wash

Lay out paper, a palette, a water container, a rag and three brushes—one for mixing, one for painting and one for pulling up puddles of extra paint—within easy reach. Use a separate brush to mix the paint so you won't have undiluted clumps of pigment on the brush you're using for painting.

Load a wide, flat brush with the paint mixture. I use a 3-inch (76mm) hake brush for 8" x 10" (20cm x 25cm) areas—the larger the area, the wider the brush. Cover as much space as possible at once. Stand when you paint washes so you have plenty of freedom of movement. Stroke across the top of the dry paper. Load the brush again and make another stroke, this time in the opposite direction and overlapping the bottom of the previous stroke by about a third. Continue this process—loading the brush and stroking back and forth down the paper until the area is covered.

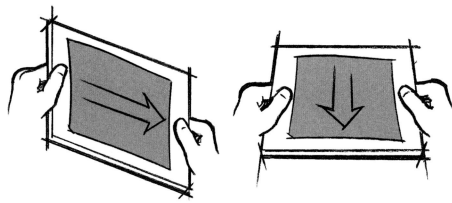

Tilting Your Paper

As long as the painted area is still very wet and hasn't started to dry yet, you can tilt your paper to even out the paint. Tilt it back and forth in whatever direction necessary to smooth out any lines. Then use a dry brush to lift any puddles of water that may have formed of the edges of the wash. This prevents the extra water from running back in. If the finished results aren't as dark as you wanted, wait for the area to dry completely and repeat the wash. A word of caution: Some cheaper papers don't absorb repeated washes well, and the paint will smear instead.

Applying a Gradated Wash

A gradated wash changes value. You must work quickly to complete the wash before any part of it dries.

Work on a wash from light to dark. If you try to apply a gradated wash from dark to light, you'll waste precious time cleaning the dark color out of your brush before moving on to the lighter value. If you want a wash to go from dark to light, turn your paper upside down and paint from light to dark.

To save much needed time, make a big gradated mixture on your palette before you start painting. First, make a big puddle of clear water at the top of the palette. Then, make a big puddle of a dark mixture at the bottom of the palette. Join the two puddles in the middle to make one mixture that gradates from almost clear water to a dark mixture.

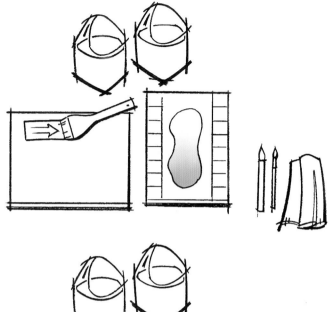

Start With Water
Lay out your supplies the same way you did for a flat wash, using two water containers instead of one. Use the water on the left for making the mixture and the water on the right for cleaning your brushes. Load a wide, flat brush with clear water. While standing, stroke the brush across the dry paper.

Add Some Color
Load the brush again, this time from the top portion of the puddle on your palette.

Gradual Transition
Apply the paint and water mixture so the wash begins as mostly water and gradates to more and more color.

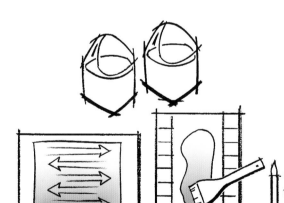

Add More Color As You Go
Make another stroke in the opposite direction, overlapping the bottom of the previous stroke by about a third. Continue this process—loading the brush and stroking back and forth from the top to the bottom of the paper. As long as the painted area is still very wet and hasn't begun to dry, smooth the wash by tilting your paper. Lift up any puddles at the edges with a dry brush to prevent backruns. If you want the wash to be darker, repeat it after the first wash has dried.

Applying a Variegated Wash

A variegated wash changes from one color to another, with the two colors blending in the middle.

Just as you mixed a gradated wash on your palette, mix a variegated wash before painting. Make a big puddle of the first paint mixture at the top of the palette. In the example on this page, I used Prussian blue. Wash out your brush and make another puddle of the second paint mixture at the bottom of the palette. I used alizarin crimson in this example. Join the puddles so the two colors bleed together to make one big puddle of paint that gradates from blue to purple to crimson.

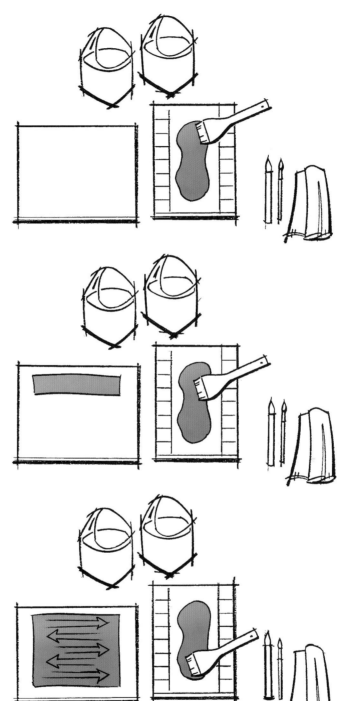

Multiple Transitions
A variegated wash changes from one color to another, blending the two in the middle.

Start With One Color
Lay out your supplies as you did for the gradated wash, including two water containers. Load a clean, wide flat brush from the top of the paint mixture.

Continue With More Color
While standing, stroke the brush across the dry paper. Then load the brush from a slightly lower part of the puddle.

Smooth Out the Wash
Make another stroke in the opposite direction, overlapping the bottom of the previous stroke by about a third. Continue this process—loading the brush from the palette, from the top down, and stroking back and forth to the bottom of the paper. As long as the area hasn't begun to dry, smooth out the wash by tilting your paper. Lift any puddles at the edges to prevent back runs. If the finished results aren't as dark as you'd like, repeat the wash after the first one has dried completely.

Something's Wrong With My Wash

So you've been practicing, and your wash just didn't turn out like you thought it would. Here are some pitfalls artists often fall into. Once you've identified the problem, keep practicing until you get it right.

Unwanted Streaks and Lines Appeared
Unwanted streaks and lines appear if you try to cover a large area with a brush that is too small. Work quickly with as large a brush as possible so the wash won't start to dry before you're finished.

Paint Dried Unevenly
Starting in the middle of the area you want to cover makes your job harder than it has to be. The paint on the outer edge starts to dry before the paint in the middle. If you overlap the edge with a stroke of wet paint, the edge of the first stroke will show. Each area should dry at the same time. Start at a corner and work outward so you won't have to overlap old strokes.

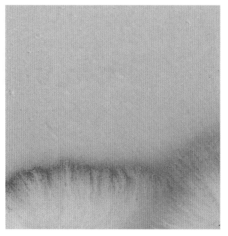

Watermarks From Backruns Occurred
Puddles of excess fluid left at the edges of a wash can run back into the area starting to dry and cause watermarks. Touch the tip of a dry brush—sometimes called a thirsty brush—to the puddle while the paper is still wet to lift the extra fluid from the paper. Dry the brush with a rag and repeat as many times as necessary. Be careful not to smear any paint that has begun to settle.

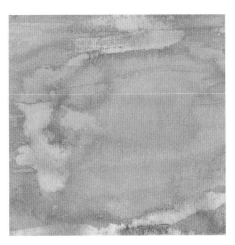

Paint Smeared

Watercolors are not like oils or acrylics. Brushing the paint once it begins to settle can smear the paint. Once watercolor paint starts to dry, it's out of your hands. Don't overwork it.

Second Wash Repelled Color

Applying another wash before the previous one has dried may smear or repel the color from the first wash. Make sure each wash is completely dry before starting another one.

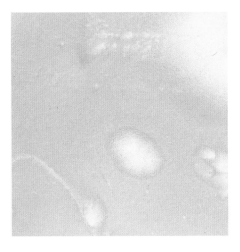

UFO's Have Invaded

"Unwanted Foreign Objects," such as dust, lint, cat hair and oil from fingerprints, cause streaks and spots if they end up in your wash before it dries. Make sure anything that comes in contact with the paper, such as paint, a rag or brushes, is clean before you use it, and don't handle the surface of the paper any more than you have to.

Positive and Negative Painting

Negative painting is an easy technique to learn when painting with watercolors. You just need to plan ahead. You might paint the negative space of an object around a white area or over a previous wash of color. It's easy to plan what areas to leave untouched if indicating a white object, such as white water in rapids. Take the challenge of painting an object that normally is brown, such as a fence, by leaving the fence white and painting the shapes around it.

You can make a dull, drab fence into an interesting part of your composition. Use negative painting as a way to present an ordinary image in a unique way. I like to imply the shapes of daisies on a dark background using negative painting.

negative painting   positive painting

Imply Shapes

Negative painting implies an image by painting the shapes around it. Positive painting, in contrast, means simply painting the object. To paint a fence using negative painting, for instance, you'd leave the white of the paper for the fence and define the fence's shape by painting the colors of the foliage behind it. To paint the fence positively, the brushstrokes themselves should indicate the fence posts and rails. Carefully plan your composition before painting. Draw all of the shapes in lightly, then paint around the object, only implying its shape.

Painting Straight Lines

You can use a straight edge, such as a ruler, to make long, straight lines. Following the edge with a round brush, as you would with a pencil, can cause the paint to spill under the ruler with unpredictable results. Instead, follow the technique below.

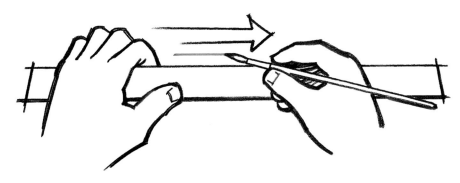

Steadying Your Hand

Prop up the ruler with the hand you don't paint with, resting your fingers between the surface and the back of the ruler. Place your thumb along the front of the ruler to stabilize it. The top edge of the ruler should be elevated while the bottom edge rests on the paper.

Next, load a no. 2 or no. 6 round brush with paint. Place the ferrule, or metal part, of the brush so it rests on the ruler's edge. Paint the line by dropping the tip of the brush to the surface of the paper. If you're right-handed, start at the left and pull the line to the right. If you're left-handed, start at the right and pull the line to the left. Let the ferrule ride along the edge of the ruler.

Using Straight Lines in a Painting

I painted most of this scene loosely, but the contrast of the straight lines on the blades really brings the focus to the windmill and makes a bold statement. The straight lines make the mill look much more realistic than freehand lines would indicate.

Creating Texture

You can create texture by moving or disbursing paint while it's still wet. The results vary depending on the type of paper you use and how damp you make the paper. Experiment on scrap watercolor paper before trying any of these techniques on a painting. Keep your practice scraps and trim them to be used as bookmarks or note-cards. Applying textures can be great fun, but texture shouldn't be the main attraction of a painting. Instead it should enhance the overall theme.

Adding More Water
Apply a wash of color and let it stand until almost dry. Then touch the tip of a round brush loaded with water onto the wet surface. This water will push away the previously applied wet paint. This technique works well for elements like the leaves above. To emphasize contrast in these areas, you can use a tissue to carefully blot the center of a freshly painted area.

Adding More Paint
Rather than applying more water, you can apply a paint mixture. The mixture will push away the previously applied wet paint. This is similar to painting wet-on-wet, except now you'll wait until the paint from the previous wash is almost dry before applying a second color. The colors won't blend smoothly as in a wet-on-wet wash, but instead they'll push against each other to create unique textural effects. Experiment on scraps of watercolor paper to be certain of the results before using this technique in a painting.

Adding Salt

Hold grains of salt between your thumb and forefinger and drop them onto the wet surface of a freshly applied wash. Be patient. The effect doesn't always appear immediately. The salt continues to work its magic until the wash dries completely. Don't use a hair dryer to speed up drying time, though. When the wash is dry, gently wipe away remaining salt crystals. Bigger salt grains, such as coarse kosher salt and rock salt, leave bigger splotches than regular table salt.

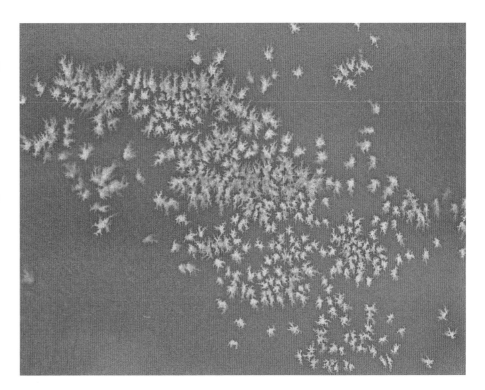

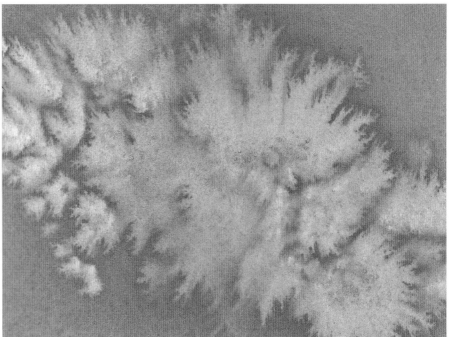

Use Different Amounts of Water
The results can vary depending on the dampness of the paper. In the example top, I added table salt once the wash looked like a thin sheen. The wash above practically had puddles when I added the table salt. Experiment adding salt at varying levels of dampness. The wetter the wash, the more the salt spreads and dissolves, which results in a subtle texture.

Lifting Paint

After you've applied a wash, you can lift some of the paint from the surface before it has dried. Professional-grade papers usually respond better to this technique.

Lifting With a Tissue
While the wash is still damp, bunch up a facial tissue, press it firmly against the paper and quickly pull it away to lift some of the paint. This technique works well for clouds, for example.

Lifting With a Paintbrush
Drag an old, dry brush over a wash of color that is nearly dry. The pressure you need to use could damage a good brush. This technique works well to paint weathered wood.

Spattering

Random dots can add a rustic feel to a watering can or imply the texture of sand on a beach. Practice on a scrap piece of paper to get used to the results. Use scrap paper to cover any area where you don't want the dots to land.

Indicating Sand

Spattering with two paintbrushes produces fewer dots, but they're bigger. Spattering with a comb and a toothbrush produces lots of small dots. I painted the dots above using two brushes.

Return From Fishing
7½" x 13"
(19cm x 33cm)
140-lb. (300gsm) cold-press watercolor paper

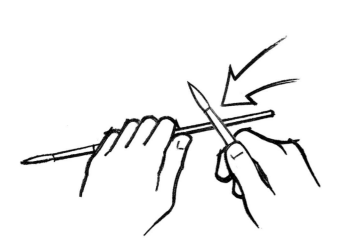

Two Paintbrushes

Gently tap one paintbrush loaded with paint against the handle of another paintbrush.

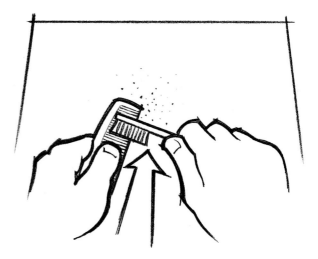

Toothbrush and Comb

Instead of brushes, you can also use a toothbrush and comb. Load the toothbrush with paint and drag it over the teeth of a comb with the tip pointed toward the watercolor paper.

Applying a Wrap

Placing some nonabsorbent material, such as plastic wrap or aluminum foil, over wet paint gives an impression of marble.

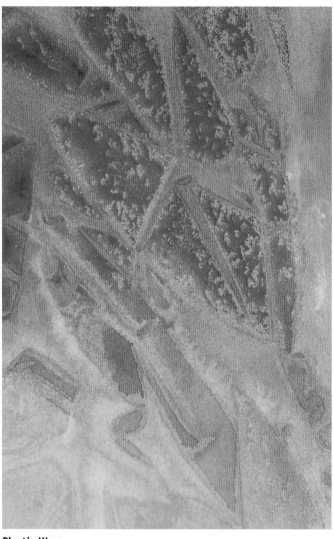

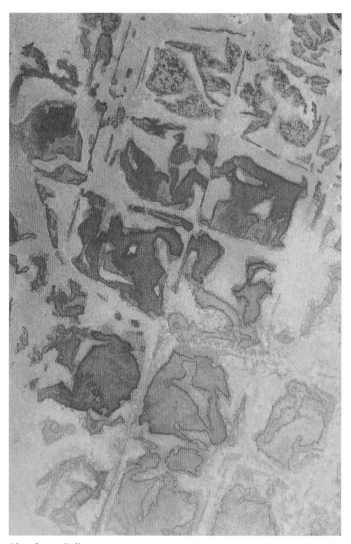

Plastic Wrap

Lay crumpled plastic wrap over a thick puddle of paint sitting on the paper. Let it dry for several hours before removing the plastic wrap. For softer, less defined edges, pull the wrap up before the paint dries completely.

Aluminum Foil

Aluminum foil also works, but you won't be able to see the results until you lift it off. Foil doesn't cling to a wet surface like plastic wrap does, so I place a heavy book on top of it to make a good impression. You can either crease the foil to make straight lines or crumple it for a marble effect.

Stenciling and Imprinting

Use your imagination to think of household items you can use to create texture. To stencil, place an item, such as an onion or potato bag, over the surface and paint over it. To imprint a texture, apply paint to an item, such as a sponge, and then press the item onto dry paper.

Imprint

Leave an imprint on the paper by pressing an item, such as a sponge, that is loaded with paint against a dry surface. You can apply an imprint on blank paper or over a wash of color.

Stencil

Use large mesh material, such as an onion bag, as a stencil to make a patterned effect. Load a 1-inch (25mm) flat brush that has firm bristles with a paint mixture. While holding the flat onion bag firmly in place, drag the brush over the bag. You can use stenciling to add a patterned texture to something like this basket.

Matting and Framing

A watercolor painting isn't complete without a mat and frame. Correctly matching a mat and frame to the composition of your painting will dramatically enhance it.

Use the table on page 63 as a guide for the sizes of mats and frames to use for your paintings. This information is based on standard paper, mat and frame sizes. The image size is the amount of the paper that will show after you've matted the painting. It's OK to paint bigger than this and let the mat crop the scene for you.

If you're painting on 9" x 12" (23cm x 30cm) paper, for instance, an 11" x 14" (28cm x 36cm) mat will work well and allow an 8" x 10" (20cm x 25cm) area to show through. Or if you want a framed picture that is 12" x 16" (30cm x 41cm), go backwards through the chart to see that you should paint on 10" x 14" (25cm x 36cm) or 12" x 16" (30cm x 41cm) paper, and a 9" x 12" (23cm x 30cm) part of the image will show. You also can have mats custom cut to fill a frame or fit the paper you're working on.

Like paper, mat board that isn't acid free will yellow with age. Make sure you look for the acid-free label. If a picture is worth framing, it's worth the cost of acid-free mat board.

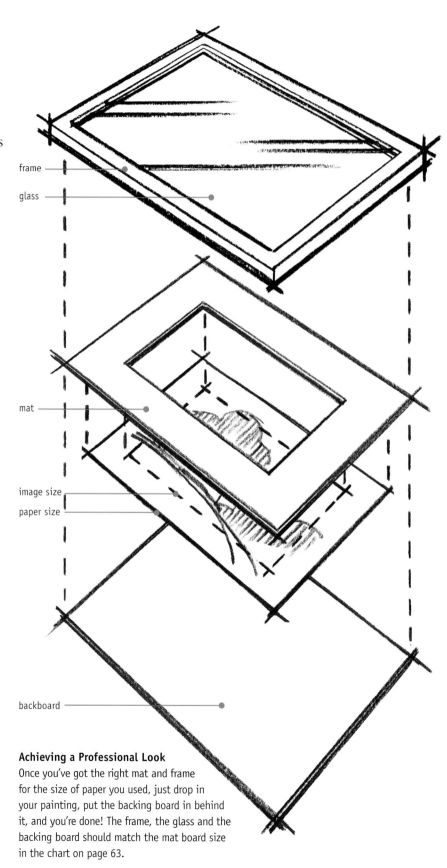

frame

glass

mat

image size

paper size

backboard

Achieving a Professional Look
Once you've got the right mat and frame for the size of paper you used, just drop in your painting, put the backing board in behind it, and you're done! The frame, the glass and the backing board should match the mat board size in the chart on page 63.

A Beginner's Efforts

I am the painter of this pair, and Mary considers herself an absolute beginner when it comes to watercolor, so we thought it would be helpful for you to see the result of Mary's efforts from the demonstration on page 72. She's proud enough of what she was able to do with the help of my demonstration to show the painting to some of her friends.

A Beginner's Professional Results

Look at the difference a mat and frame makes in creating a professional-looking product. Mary painted the 8" x 10" (20cm x 25cm) image on 10" x 14" (25cm x 36cm) paper and framed and matted it with an 11" x 14" (28cm x 36cm) mat and frame.

Camargo Gatehouse
Mary Willenbrink
8" x 10" (20cm x 25cm)
140-lb. (300gsm) cold-press watercolor paper

What Size Mat and Frame Do I Need?

Paper Size	Image Size	Mat and Frame Size
4" x 6" (10cm x 15cm)	3½" x 5" (9cm x 13cm)	5" x 7" (13cm x 18cm)
7" x 10" (18cm x 25cm)	5" x 7" (13cm x 18cm)	8" x 10" (20cm x 25cm)
9" x 12" (23cm x 30cm)	8" x 10" (20cm x 25cm)	11" x 14" (28cm x 36cm)
10" x 14" (25cm x 36cm)	8" x 10" (20cm x 25cm)	11" x 14" (28cm x 36cm)
10" x 14" (25cm x 36cm)	9" x 12" (23cm x 30cm)	12" x 16" (30cm x 41cm)
12" x 16" (30cm x 41cm)	9" x 12" (23cm x 30cm)	12" x 16" (30cm x 41cm)
14" x 20" (36cm x 51cm)	11" x 14" (28cm x 36cm)	16" x 20" (41cm x 51cm)

Discussing Techniques

Paint Techniques

I started this painting with the background, using a wet-on-wet technique. Then I concentrated on the foreground. I used a wet-on-wet technique for the first layer and then applied additional layers of paint, using the wet-on-dry technique. I used a straight edge to paint straight lines on elements like the edges of the roof. I used negative painting to paint around the house. Value contrasts between light and dark areas and color contrasts between the bright colors of the background and the neutral colors of the house contribute to an interesting composition. This mansion was once a status symbol in its grandiosity and now is in shambles, which, in itself, is a contrast. With this painting, I was trying to convey that the things of this world are only temporary.

Victorian Repose
18" x 14" (46cm x 36cm)
140-lb. (300gsm) cold-press watercolor paper

Negative Painting

I drew a structural drawing and then used my finest brushes to control my paints. Negative painting played a big role, expressing what is going on around the deer, especially the distinct forms of the tree branches that add to the composition. I used a limited palette of browns and greens, providing variation in the values of these colors to give the painting a natural feel of the outdoors. The name of this painting expresses the surprise of both the viewer and the deer, who seem to notice each other simultaneously.

Spotted
10" x 14" (25cm x 36cm)
140-lb. (300gsm) hot-press watercolor paper

Stained Glass Effect

The lead framework on stained glass usually is a dark color, but leaving it white lets the viewer concentrate on the vibrant, transparent colors, a characteristic shared by stained glass and watercolor paint.

King of Kings
7" x 4" (18cm x 10cm)
140-lb. (300gsm) hot-press watercolor paper

Living Sacrifice
7" x 4" (18cm x 10cm)
140-lb. (300gsm) hot-press watercolor paper

Let's Paint

Painting with watercolors is fun, and it's even more exciting when you learn the techniques unique to this particular medium. In this chapter you'll practice some easy techniques that will bring more creativity, interest and enjoyment to your watercolor paintings and experiences.

Before each demonstration, you'll find a list of materials you'll need to complete each painting. You'll also see the image size listed. The image size is the part of the painting that will show if you mat and frame the painting. I've also listed the lessons from the book that you'll use in each demonstration. Glance back to those pages to refresh your memory before starting a painting or when you reach a trouble spot during the painting. Have fun!

Getting Ready

As we were writing this book together, we kept in mind that we were writing for you, the absolute beginner. I am a professional artist and a teacher, but teaming up with Mary, an absolute beginner herself, as a cowriter helped. Often, Mary would ask questions you might have asked if you were in one of my classes: "How did you do that?" "Why did you do this first?" "Can you talk me through this demonstration?" "Why don't my colors look like yours?" Then we tried to include answers in the book for your benefit.

Prepare Your Work Area
Make sure all of your supplies are within reach before you start painting; watercolors sometimes demand you work quickly. You'll find a comprehensive list of painting and drawing supplies on page 15. You'll also find materials specific to each painting on the first page of each demonstration. Make sure your work area is clean and dry; it's essential to a peaceful, stress-free painting session.

Prepare Your Mind
Remember to have fun with watercolors! Because they're unpredictable, some artists feel tense and out of control at first. You just have to approach watercolor painting with the appropriate mindset: Let the watercolors behave as the transparent, fluid paints they are. Let them do their thing. You may be surprised and enjoy the results.

Also keep the tips mentioned at the beginning of each demo in your mind as you paint. I'm teaching you how to paint from afar. In an actual class, I would remind you, for instance, "Remember where your light source is coming from as you lay this wash! Look for some of the whites in the painting." I can't be there to do that for you as you paint these demos, so train yourself to remember these things as you paint.

A Bit of Praise
As an instructor, I also like to comment on the positive aspects of your work as you're painting. I wish I could be there to point out the neat and unique things I can see about your painting. Encouragement is a major part of the painting process.

Don't be humble. Appreciate the successes in each painting you do. Remember that inconsistencies aren't mistakes, there will be nuances in your work. Don't forget to encourage and praise yourself. You deserve it.

Date Your Paintings
Dating your paintings will give you a creative diary of your progress. I like to go through my old paintings every once in a while, and I actually enjoy them more after they've been set aside a few months.

You may not always like a painting when you finish it. Maybe the composition didn't turn out as you planned or maybe you feel you

went too dark with the background colors. A few weeks later, though, you may find you're actually growing in your talents. Perhaps you've finally moved away from colors that are too muted. You may have trouble recognizing and appreciating growth in your own work. Keep your paintings for awhile; you may find that they grow on you.

Great Aunt Harriet
Consider matting and framing each painting. It's amazing what it can do to a simple watercolor. Although you may not always appreciate your end results, art is in the eye of the beholder. Someone else may view your painting altogether differently. Something in the composition may have special meaning to him or her, or someone like your Great Aunt Harriet may simply love it because she loves you.

Keep It Clean
Food crumbs and oils from your fingers can affect the way paint lays on your paper—so it's probably a good idea not to eat fried chicken while you paint!

Structural Drawing

In this demonstration, you'll create a structural drawing by sketching the simple shapes of a gatehouse. Take the time to draw straight, parallel lines with a straight edge.

This drawing will be the foundation for the next two watercolor demonstrations. You can either draw a structural drawing directly onto watercolor paper or draw the image on sketch paper and then trace or transfer it to watercolor paper once you're satisfied with the drawing. I prefer to draw an image on sketch paper at whatever size is comfortable. I use a photocopier to enlarge or reduce the drawing to the size I want to paint and then I transfer my drawing onto watercolor paper.

Each step in this demonstration adds basic shapes that will provide the structure for your paintings. The layered shapes will make up a complete scene.

Materials List

Paper
10" x 14" (25cm x 36cm) 140-lb. (300gsm) cold-press watercolor paper

Other
kneaded eraser
2B pencil

Lessons & Techniques

Structural drawing (page 21)
Measuring (page 22)

Tips

Take the time to create a sound drawing. It's the secret to painting a beautiful watercolor you will be proud of for years to come.

Don't worry about including too many details now. You can leave some, such as the details on the foliage, for the painting stage.

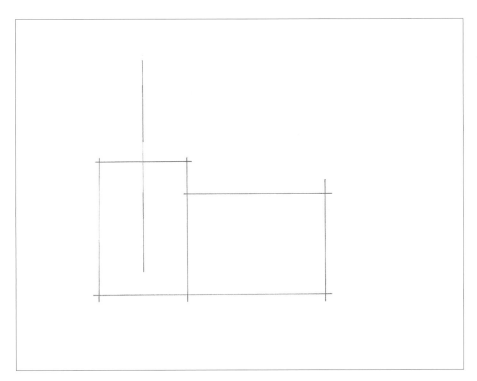

1 Draw Basic Structure of House

Draw two rectangles to create the base of the house with a 2B pencil. The bottom line should be a few inches from the bottom of your paper. Sketch a vertical dividing line through the left rectangle to help you keep things balanced.

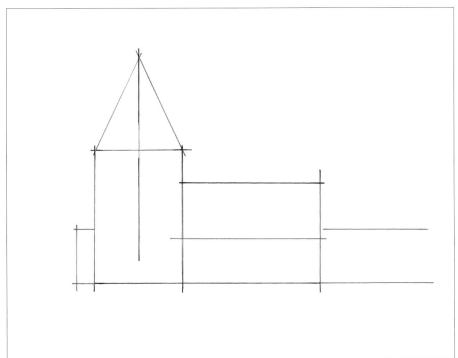

2 Draw Roofs

Add slanted lines over the first rectangle to make a triangle that will form the peak of the roof. Divide the right rectangle horizontally to indicate the roof of this part of the house. Add a rectangle on each side of the picture, creating the wall.

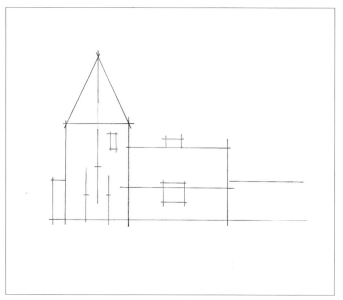

3 Draw Accents
Sketch the windows, chimney and sides of the door. Draw a line to indicate where the top of the door will be.

4 Draw Curved Lines
Add the curves on the door and roof, and start detailing the windows.

5 Add Details
Add trim details to the windows and slate roof, and draw some stones on the walls of the gatehouse.

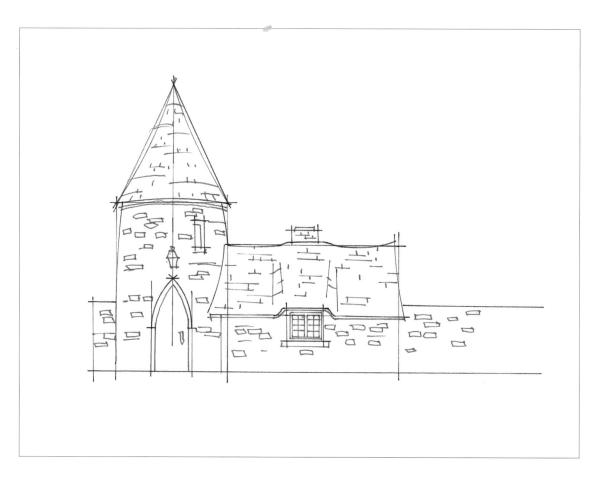

6 Draw Foliage
Indicate the basic shape of the foliage.

7 Add Finishing Touches
Finish by drawing the outline of the trees and shrubs, throwing in a few stones on the walkway and a bit of grass. You can leave the details of the foliage for your watercolors.

Now erase any unnecessary lines, such as the dividing lines that helped you draw the rooftops. On any painting, erase any unnecessary pencil lines before painting. They will be more difficult to erase once you've painted over them.

Painting With One Color

In this demonstration you'll examine the lights and darks of the scene. Concentrating on this aspect of painting, especially in watercolors, will help you master values and colors for later demonstrations. It's truly rewarding to show people a finished painting and be able to tell them that the white areas are actually the white of the paper. It shows people that you planned this painting and have the skills to follow through.

If you drew the gatehouse from the last demonstration on watercolor paper, you're ready to paint! If you drew the image on sketch paper so as not to ruin the watercolor paper with lots of erasing and redrawing, trace or transfer the image onto your watercolor paper. Unless you're using a watercolor paper block, secure all four sides of your paper to a mounting board with sealing tape.

Materials List

Paper
10" x 14" (25cm x 36cm) 140-lb. (300gsm)
    cold-press watercolor paper
Image Size for Matting and Framing
8" x 10" (20cm x 25cm)

Paint
burnt umber or sepia

Brushes
no. 2 round
no. 6 round
no. 10 round
large bamboo

Other
value scale

Lessons & Techniques

Understanding Value (page 26)
Following the Painting Process (page 38)
Mixing Paint and Handling Brushes (page 45)
Painting Wet-on-Dry (page 48)
Positive and Negative Painting (page 54)

Tips

Keep a value scale close by as you paint or even make one using the same color you're painting with. Remember that watercolor will look lighter after it dries. Don't be discouraged if a wash doesn't look like it's supposed to. Consider it a learning experience. Let each wash dry before applying the next one. Start with general shapes and value masses and then move on to painting fine details later. Make the background darker than the gatehouse so the building's shape is clear and well defined. Keep your light source in mind as you paint. As you paint in the details, leave a bit for the imagination. Just imply texture in some places rather than painting each stone on the walls, each leaf on the trees and each blade of grass.

1 Paint Background

Paint the background leaves with a large bamboo brush. Turn the painting sideways to make it easier for you to paint around the gatehouse.

2 Paint Building

Make a mixture with a liberal amount of water to create a value lighter than the background. Add this color to the building to contrast the dark background with a no. 10 round brush. Leave some areas white to appear as highlights, paying attention to the light source shining from the upper left.

3 Paint Foreground

Make a paint mixture that is a bit darker than the building. Sweep the paint across the foreground ivy, shrubs and grass with a bamboo brush. At this point, don't worry about defining these elements; just block in the general values of the area.

4 Add Darks to Background

The darkest value so far should be the background. Layer a darker value over some areas of the leaves with a no. 10 round brush. This will add depth to the foliage.

5 Add Midtones to Building

Add washes of color over several parts of the building with a no. 10 round. Make the value slightly darker than the first washes on the building.

6 Suggest Details in Foreground

Make some mixtures that are slightly darker than the first foreground wash. Apply washes of these mixtures in the foreground with a no. 10 round to suggest bushes, ivy and grass.

7 Add Another Layer of Washes

Add darker washes to the background to better define the trees and leaves with a no. 10 round. Indicate the tree trunks by painting the negative shapes around the trunks with a darker wash. Add a few dark accents to the building, including the window on the tower, the door, the eaves and some dark areas on the roof, with a no. 6 round. Remember to paint around small detail areas that will remain light, such as the handle on the door. Also add some definition to the vegetation in front of the building with a no. 6 round.

The Gatehouse
8" x 10" (20cm x 25cm)
140-lb. (300gsm) cold-press watercolor paper

Painting With

This demonstration will show you ju

ited palette. We'll use only the three

ors represented in this scene. You'll

first demonstration as you will have

You'll be layering washes of differ

es of different values in the last dem.

the background, building and foregro

before adding a new wash so paint c

ors. You can use a hair dryer to spee

haven't left any puddles of water, wh

of the air. You can lift puddles with

Tips

Spend the extra money to bu

low. You'll be mixing a bright yel

cadmium yellow will not do the jc

foreground washes are mixtures

blue. As the washes get darker, a

of alizarin crimson to the darkes

neutral and natural. To get a

yellow, alizarin crimson and Pruss

is dominant in this mixture, add a

ry color to make it more neutral.

too red, add green (yellow + blu

water until you get the right valu

by to help control and mix your

about the color and value of a m

a scrap piece of watercolor pap

Watercolors don't allow do-ove

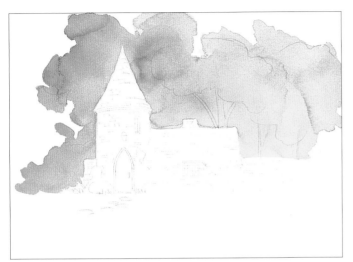

1 Paint Background

Make a few different yellow-green mixtures of light value from cadmium yellow and Prussian blue. Apply washes of these mixtures to the background with a bamboo brush.

2 Paint Building

Make a few different brown and gray mixtures of light value (see the tip on page 76). Before you lay any paint down, plan which parts of the paper will be white so you can preserve the white of the paper for these areas. Refer to the monochromatic painting you just finished to help you plan. Apply washes of these mixtures for the stones, brick chimney and slate roof with a no. 10 round brush.

3 Paint Foreground

Lay down light, yellow-green washes for the foreground shapes with a bamboo brush. Add more cadmium yellow to the mixture for the grass, and add more Prussian blue for the ivy and shrubs.

4 Add Midtones to Background

Add more Prussian blue and a small amount of alizarin crimson to your yellow-green mixture. Remembering that your light source is coming from the upper left, lay down some darker washes with a no. 10 round brush.

5 Add Midtones to Building

Make slightly darker brown and gray mixtures and paint over the lighter washes on the building with a no. 10 round. Leave some areas from the first layer of washes untouched. The building should now have three values; the white of the paper, the first layer of washes and some areas with the second wash layered on top of the first.

6 Add Midtones to Foreground

Darken the ivy and shrubs with more green and add some slightly darker washes of yellow-green in the grass with a no. 10 round.

7 Add Darks

Add a few washes of a dark blue-green mixture to the background with a no. 10 round. To mix a dark blue-green, start with a regular green mixture—cadmium yellow and Prussian blue. Add small amounts of blue. Mix the color thick and rich on the palette, adding one brush full of water at a time until it is a good consistency to work with. If your paints have dried too much for you to mix them before adding water, use fresh paint.

Layer darker gray and brown washes on the building, and paint dark areas like the window, door and shadow under the eaves with a no. 6 round. Add splashes of green to the foreground with a no. 6 round.

The Gatehouse in Summer
8" x 10" (20cm x 25cm)
140-lb. (300gsm) cold-press watercolor paper

8 Add Details

Paint in the dark and light details with no. 2 and no. 6 round brushes. Erase unwanted pencil lines after the painting is completely dry. Don't forget to sign your name and date your painting!

Positive Painting

Trees are beautiful to paint, and each one has its own character. A tree can add to the composition of an outdoor scene or stand alone in its own painting. This demonstration provides an easy, fun way to make graceful, interesting trees.

I chose to paint the trees void of leaves as stark silhouettes against a flaming sunset. I love to paint trees during all four seasons because each season seems to bring out a different aspect of trees. These trees are set in autumn. The analogous warm colors of the background contrast the stark, cold feeling of the tree. I also angled the wet-on-wet background strokes to add interest.

Tips

The paper will need to be wet for steps 1 through 4. Make sure you have all of your supplies at hand, and be ready to work quickly. Use a large brush to apply the wet-on-wet washes to save time. After you've finished laying down your wet-on-wet washes and the paint has dried, you'll notice that the colors have become much more muted. After gaining some experience, you'll learn to anticipate and plan for these changes. Draw the trunks of the trees first, then all the large limbs, then the medium size branches, then the smallest ones. This yields a more natural, pleasing composition. Placing the tree trunks to the side of the painting and overlapping the branches also aids the composition, creating interesting negative space and making the trees look more natural.

Materials List

Paper
12" x 16" (30cm x 41cm) 300-lb. (640gsm) cold-press watercolor paper
Image Size for Matting and Framing
11" x 14" (28cm x 36cm)

Paints
alizarin crimson
cadmium orange
cadmium red
cadmium yellow (professional grade)
cerulean blue
Prussian blue

Brushes
no. 2 round
no. 6 round
no. 10 round
3-inch (76mm) hake
large bamboo brush

Other
spray bottle

Lessons & Techniques

Using Analogous Colors (page 31)
Planning Composition (page 34)
Painting Wet-on-Wet (page 46)
Positive Painting (page 54)

1 Begin Background
Because you'll be painting the first four steps wet-on-wet, you'll need to work quickly before the paper or paint starts to dry. Make the following mixtures of paint and water before wetting your paper: cadmium yellow, cadmium orange, cadmium red and a purple mixture of alizarin crimson and cerulean blue.

Now wet down the paper with water from a spray bottle, and even it out with a 3-inch (76mm) hake brush so the paper is covered with an even sheen of water. Try to avoid puddles of water. Apply angled streaks of cadmium yellow with a 3-inch (76mm) hake brush.

2 Add Orange
Add cadmium orange with a 3-inch (76mm) hake brush using the same angled strokes. Once the colors have dried, notice how similar the orange and yellow appear. Colors are more vivid when the paint is wet. Keep that in mind as you paint.

3 Add Red
Add cadmium red.

4 Add Some Interest
Add the purple color that you mixed from alizarin crimson and cerulean blue with a 3-inch (76mm) hake brush. Then sit back and take a deep breath. You've finished the wet-on-wet part of the painting.

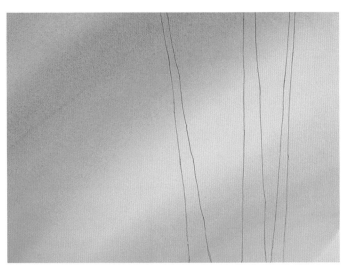

5 Draw Trees
After the paint has dried, lightly draw the thickest parts of the trees. Sometimes it's hard to erase pencil lines after you lay a wash of paint over them, so it's easier to draw the structure of the tree over the background washes. Notice that each tree is thicker at the bottom and thinner at the top.

6 Add Limbs
Add limbs, again making sure they taper as they grow away from the trunks.

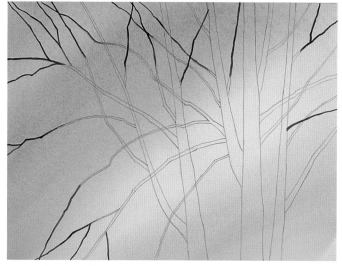

7 Finish Structural Drawing
Add the rest of the branches.

8 Paint Smallest Branches
Paint the thinnest branches with a no. 2 round and a dark mixture of Prussian blue and a slight amount of alizarin crimson.

9 Finish Trees
Paint the medium size branches with a no. 6 round, the largest branches with a no. 10 round and the trunks with a bamboo brush. When the paint has dried completely, erase any visible pencil lines and sign and date the painting.

Autumn Sunset
11" x 14"
(28cm x 36cm)
300-lb. (640gsm)
cold-press watercolor paper

Negative Painting

Painting around an object to imply its shape is a pleasant change of pace. If you enjoy doing this painting, try to incorporate negative painting into a composition of your own. Whether you use it in most of your paintings, some of them or just as a creativity exercise, negative painting enhances your composition skills and techniques. I used hot-press paper for this painting because the sharp, clean edges that result work well with the subject matter.

Remember: You don't need a bad attitude to produce a negative painting.

Tips

For a beginner, negative painting can seem intimidating and time-consuming. To make this demonstration easier, I've made the image size half the size of the positive painting demonstration. This demonstration requires detail painting. Make sure you're using brushes that form good points. Practice dropping salt into wet washes on a scrap piece of paper before trying it on your painting. Dropping salt into paint that is too dry, too wet or too thick will have little effect. Be patient; the results may be most noticeable once the paint and salt are almost dry. But don't use a hair dryer to make this part of the painting dry more quickly. It will block the salt's effect. If you're painting over another color, let the paint dry before moving on to the next step. If you're not careful, the colors will bleed and you won't have a tree anymore!

Materials List

Paper
7" x 10" (18cm x 25cm) 140-lb. (300gsm)
   hot-press watercolor paper
Image Size for Matting and Framing
5" x 7" (13cm x 18cm)

Paints
burnt sienna
Prussian blue
yellow ochre

Brushes
no. 2 round
no. 6 round
no. 10 round

Other
table salt

Lessons & Techniques

Structural Drawing (page 21)
Understanding Color (page 30)
Understanding Color Temperature (page 32)
Mixing Paint and Handling Brushes (page 45)
Negative Painting (page 54)
Creating Texture (page 56)

Avoid Large, Unbroken Spaces

Don't draw your trees like this. Instead, continue the branches beyond the image area. The branches on the left of this image end within the dimensions of the painting. I would have to paint the entire area on the left at once, which might leave unwanted lines if I paint over an area that already has started to dry. Instead, plan medium size, easy-to-paint areas in the drawing stage. The drawing in step 1 right provides an easier guide to follow as you lay paint down.

1 Draw Structure

Draw the trees as you did in the previous demonstration, starting with the thickest parts and moving on to the thin, tapered branches.

2 Paint Trees

Make separate pale mixtures of Prussian blue, burnt sienna and yellow ochre. To make a pale mixture, touch the paint with the very tip of your brush and put the paint on the palette. Add enough water to make a good size puddle. With so much water and so little paint, the mixture should be a very light value. Paint the trees with a no. 6 round, starting with blue at the bottom, fading up to a warm, light brown, then to the yellow ochre and finally to the white of the paper. The trees should be mostly white with just a bit of color.

3 Begin Background and Add Salt

Make a variegated mixture of Prussian blue and burnt sienna on your palette so you can pick up a variety of these two colors as you paint. Wipe other puddles of color off your palette. Make a large, dark mixture of burnt sienna at the bottom and another large, dark mixture of Prussian blue at the top of your palette and blend the two colors in the middle. Begin to paint in the background around the trees with no. 6 and no. 10 round brushes. Because the tree trunks will draw the viewer's attention to the right, balance the composition by concentrating the strongest, contrasting values, especially the dark blue, on the left. You'll notice that the background uses darker values of the same colors used to accent the trees. After painting a few segments of the background, drop salt into the wet paint to add more texture.

4 Add Yellow Ochre to Mix

To bring in some of the yellow from the trees, add yellow ochre to the middle of the variegated mixture on your palette and continue painting the background. Add salt as you go.

5 Don't Rush
Continue painting the background just a little at a time so you have control over the paint. Take your time adding salt to get the right effect. Don't rush yourself.

6 Continue Background
Paint a few more pieces of the background and add salt.

7 Paint Details

Once you've painted the bigger parts of the background, concentrate on the smaller, more detailed areas with a no. 2 round. Don't forget to keep adding salt.

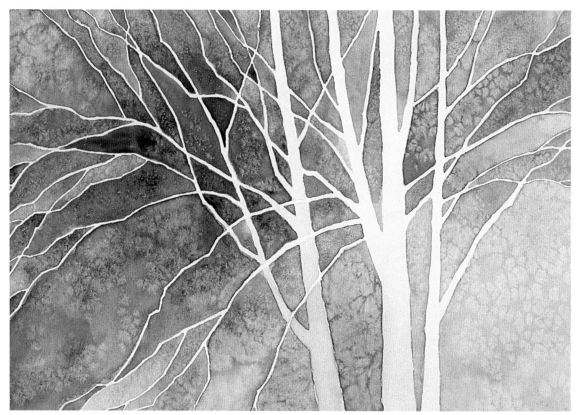

8 Add Missing Pieces

Finish painting the background with no. 2 and no. 6 rounds as if you were adding the last few pieces of a jig-saw puzzle.

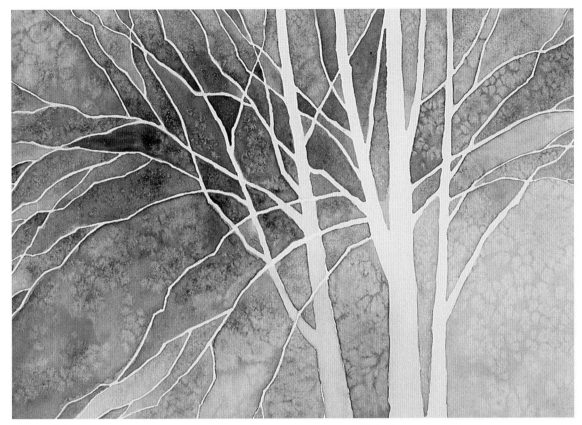

9 Finish Up

After I filled in the background and the paint dried, I stepped back to evaluate the painting. I decided to darken some of the background areas. When everything is dry, brush away the remaining salt and erase your pencil lines carefully. Sign and date your painting.

Winter Exposure
5" x 7" (13cm x 18cm)
140-lb. (300gsm) hot-press watercolor paper

Painting Flowers

You're going to get an extra drawing lesson here. You learned about linear perspective on pages 24 and 25. Perspective also applies to objects that don't have straight lines, such as the daisies in this demonstration.

To draw a circle in perspective, simply draw an ellipse. An ellipse is simply a circle viewed from an angle. Use ellipses for both the general shape of the daisy and for its center. The petals will point outward with a slight curve.

Tips

Plan your painting well during the drawing stage. Don't draw each daisy as if you were looking at it head on. Vary the perspective and tilt of each flower. Add some thickness and bulk to the flower center to keep the flower from looking flat.

Materials List

Paper
10" x 14" (25cm x 36cm) 140-lb. (300gsm)
    cold-press watercolor paper
Image Size for Matting and Framing
8" x 10" (20cm x 25cm)

Paints
alizarin crimson
cadmium orange
cadmium yellow
cerulean blue
hooker's green
Prussian blue
yellow ochre

Brushes
no. 6 round
no. 10 round

Lessons & Techniques

Structural Drawing (page 21)
Drawing Linear Perspective (page 24)
Understanding Value (page 26)
Understanding Color (page 30)
Planning Composition (page 34)
Painting Wet-on-Wet (page 46)
Painting Wet-on-Dry (page 48)
Positive and Negative Painting (page 54)

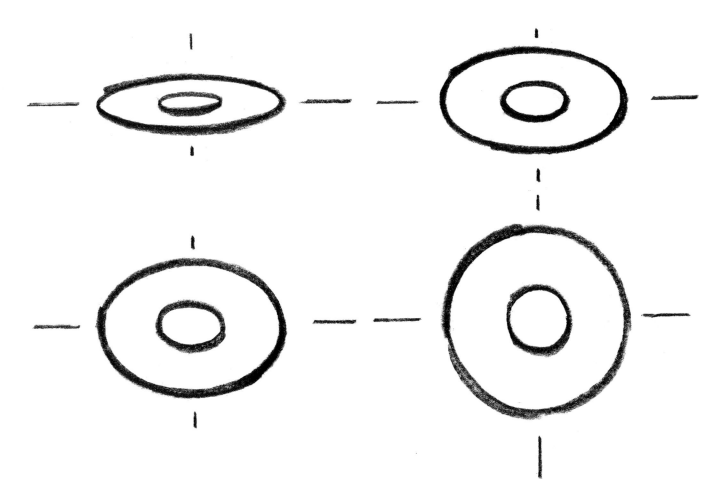

Indicating Perspective

The circles at the bottom form the base shapes of a daisy from a head-on viewpoint. The image just above represents a daisy barely leaning back. The next set of ellipses represents a daisy tilted even farther back. The daisy at the top is almost facing straight up.

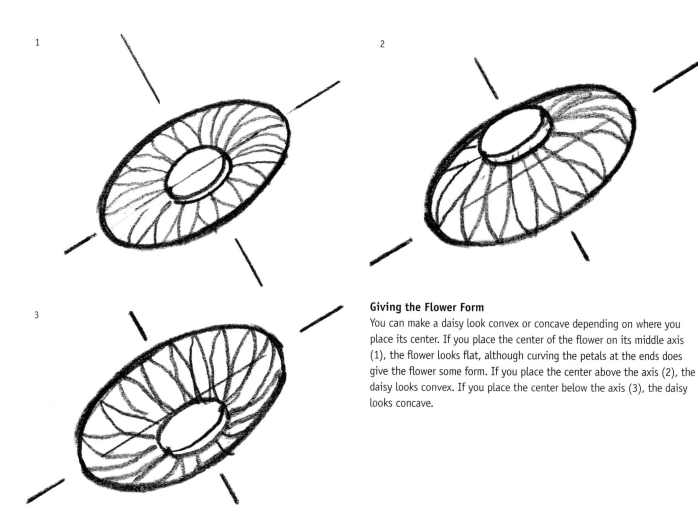

Giving the Flower Form
You can make a daisy look convex or concave depending on where you place its center. If you place the center of the flower on its middle axis (1), the flower looks flat, although curving the petals at the ends does give the flower some form. If you place the center above the axis (2), the daisy looks convex. If you place the center below the axis (3), the daisy looks concave.

1 Draw Structure
Draw the daisies at slightly varying angles. Leave some gaps between petals to add interest and a natural feel to the scene. Just roughly draw the leaves in the background. Then erase any lines that you no longer need. Once you've got the structural drawing down, you won't need the outline of each individual petal. On your watercolor paper, you might want to make your lines a bit darker than these. I realized too late that the lines for the background leaves were difficult to see after laying down my first wash of color.

2 Paint Shadows

Mix alizarin crimson and cerulean blue to make purple and then add water to the mixture. Apply it to the shadow areas of the petals with a no. 10 round. While the paint is still wet, add a few touches of a mixture of yellow ochre and cerulean blue to parts of the shadow areas to add interest. The light source is shining from the upper left and slightly behind the flowers. There are also a few shadows on the bottoms of the flowers where the petals have curved down. Don't worry if the shadows look too dark. Once you paint the background, which will define the shapes of the flowers, the shadows won't appear nearly as dark. Also remember to leave the white of the paper for the white of the flowers.

3 Paint Centers

Paint the flower centers with a no. 6 round brush and cadmium yellow. While the paint is still wet, drop in a small amount of cadmium orange and an even smaller amount of a mixture of cadmium orange and hooker's green in the middle and near the edge of each flower's center.

4 Paint Negative Shapes Around Daisies in Stages

Make puddles of the following mixtures or colors on your palette: hooker's green and Prussian blue; hooker's green and cadmium yellow; hooker's green and yellow ochre; cadmium orange and alizarin crimson. Paint small, manageable sections of the background with a no. 10 round, taking paint from various puddles on the palette. Notice how the daisies have taken shape and that the shadows no longer look as dark.

Painting a background this large is easier if you concentrate on small portions at a time. I painted the background in stages. Don't worry about hard edges resulting from applications of wet paint over a drying background. You'll paint over these when you add details to the background. Sometimes I even drop water onto the drying paint to add texture.

5 Define Background

Define the leaves with a no. 6 round brush and a mixture of a light amount of alizarin crimson and equal amounts of hooker's green and Prussian blue.

6 Finish Up

Finish the background, erase pencil lines and then sign your painting.

Shasta Parade
8" x 10" (20cm x 25cm)
140-lb. (300gsm) cold-press watercolor paper

Developing Composition

This painting's composition has three main elements, the sailboat, the house and the dinghy. The composition holds the viewer's interest because it has no elements placed directly in the center. This makes the composition seem random, though the placement of elements is actually well planned.

Tips

Review the lesson on how to paint straight lines on page 55 so you don't get frustrated; this painting has a lot of detail. If you take your time, this demonstration will reward you with a beautiful and impressive watercolor. To paint the sky, you may want to turn the picture upside down so the part you're painting is closest to you.

Materials List

Paper
10" x 14" (25cm x 36cm) 140-lb. (300gsm)
    cold-press watercolor paper
Image Size for Matting and Framing
8" x 10" (20cm x 25cm)

Paints
brown madder
hooker's green
Prussian blue
yellow ochre

Brushes
no. 2 round
no. 6 round
no. 10 round
1-inch (25mm) flat
3-inch (76mm) hake
large bamboo brush

Other
straight edge

Lessons & Techniques

Structural Drawing (page 21)
Measuring (page 22)
Understanding Value (page 26)
Painting Atmospheric Perspective (page 29)
Understanding Color (page 30)
Planning Composition (page 34)
Painting Wet-on-Dry (page 48)
Applying a Flat Wash (page 49)
Positive and Negative Painting (page 54)
Painting Straight Lines (page 55)

1 Draw Structure
Draw, trace or transfer the image onto watercolor paper.

2 Paint Sky
Wet the sky and any other area that you want to be blue with clear water and a 3-inch (76mm) hake brush. Add Prussian blue to the wet areas with a 1-inch (25mm) flat. Paint the building, boat and dinghy's shadow areas with no. 6 and no. 10 round brushes and Prussian blue. The paint will spread to any area where the paper is wet, so don't wet any area you don't want to be blue.

3 Paint Shore
Paint the shoreline with yellow ochre and brown madder and a no. 10 round. Add the trees with mixtures of yellow ochre, brown madder, hooker's green and Prussian blue.

4 Paint Water

Paint the water with Prussian blue and a no. 10 round. Use a wet-on-dry technique and work quickly. Keep the edges active. Don't let the edge of a stroke dry before adding more paint and continuing to cover the water area. Start at the upper left, painting around the boat first. Then paint around the dinghy. Switch to a large bamboo brush and work across the picture from top to bottom. The point where you started painting the water probably will have started to dry, leaving a hard edge. In this part of the painting process, that's OK. It will look like wake from the sailboat, a little detail that indicates movement and makes the painting more interesting. If you accept watercolors for the way they behave, you'll come to appreciate the effects they produce and the creativity they allow.

5 Paint Building

Paint the building and the roof with a no. 6 round and a mixture of brown madder and Prussian blue, leaving the trim white.

6 Add Details

Paint shadows in the trees and on the shore with a no. 10 round and mixtures of Prussian blue, brown madder, hooker's green and yellow ochre. Indicate tree trunks with negative painting using a darker mixture than the the trees in step 3.

7 Paint Finishing Touches

Paint the waves with a no. 10 round and a mixture of Prussian blue and brown madder. Start with small, horizontal lines at the shore and use progressively longer, more spread out strokes as you get closer to the bottom of the picture.

Paint the windows on the building and boat with a no. 2 round and Prussian blue. Emphasize the shadow and add some accents to the roof with brown madder and the same brush. Add some accents to the dinghy. Add accents to the sailboat and sail with Prussian blue, yellow ochre and brown madder, using a straight edge and a no. 2 round to paint the straight lines. Paint the curved lines on the hull with a fluid motion by moving your arm at the elbow rather than at the wrist or fingers. Add some vague shadows on the sail with a light value of Prussian blue to indicate some wind. Sign and date the painting and you're done!

Easy Going
10" x 8" (25cm x 20cm)
140-lb. (300gsm) cold-press watercolor paper

Using a Color Scheme

Pumpkins are good subject matter to paint when learning to use water-colors because they have relatively simple shapes. As my students have learned, pumpkins may not hold the beauty of roses, but they sure are a lot easier to paint! Starting simply is a valuable part of the learning process.

Tips

Limiting your palette to just four colors and using each of these in almost each element will give your painting a feeling of continuity. Even if pumpkins are orange, that orange can have a little red, yellow and blue in it. Use all four colors to paint the two outer pumpkins. Leave Prussian blue out of the mixture for the three center pumpkins until the shading stage. Because orange and blue are complements, adding blue to the predominantly orange pumpkin will make it dull. The center pumpkins will be brighter and more noticeable to the viewer's eye. Remember to plan and preserve white space and highlights. The light source is shining from the upper right. When mixing browns, use your color chart to help get the color right. If your mixture has a bit too much of one color, add a slight amount of its complement. For example, if your brown is too green, add red.

Materials List

Paper
12" x 16" (30cm x 41cm) 300-lb. (640gsm) cold-press watercolor paper
Image Size for Matting and Framing
11" x 14" (28cm x 36cm)

Paints
alizarin crimson
cadmium orange
cadmium yellow
Prussian blue

Brushes
no. 6 round
no. 10 round
large bamboo brush

Lessons & Techniques

Structural Drawing (page 21)
Measuring (page 22)
Drawing Linear Perspective (page 24)
Understanding Value (page 26)
Understanding Complementary and Analogous Colors (page 31)
Understanding Color Temperature (page 32)
Planning Composition (page 34)
Following the Painting Process (page 38)
Mixing Paint and Handling Brushes (page 45)
Painting Wet-on-Wet (page 46)
Painting Wet-on-Dry (page 48)

1 Draw Structure

Draw the basic shapes of your composition to work out the placement of your pumpkins. Vary the pumpkins' sizes and tilt some of them to create interest. Overlap them and make the pumpkins closest to the viewer appear lower in the scene. Even pumpkins have perspective! After adding the barrel and pumpkin stems, I decided my painting still needed a little something, so I added a few apples and some simple lines to indicate grass.

2 Begin Pumpkins

Draw or transfer the image onto watercolor paper. I changed the tilt of the pumpkin on the bottom left because I felt that it led the viewer's eye out of the painting. This small change will keep the viewer's eye within the frame of the picture. I decided to use orange and its analogous colors plus orange's complement, blue, for the color scheme.

Fill in the pumpkin on the left with a large bamboo brush and very wet, somewhat sloppy applications of cadmium orange. Painting wet-on-wet, drop in a mixture of alizarin crimson and cadmium yellow with a no. 6 round. Paint the stems with a brown mixture of alizarin crimson, cadmium orange, cadmium yellow and Prussian blue.

3 Continue Pumpkins

Paint the three center pumpkins with cadmium orange. Painting wet-on-wet, add some color from a mixture of alizarin crimson and cadmium yellow. Paint the pumpkin on the right the same way, adding a trace amount of Prussian blue to the mixture. Remember to preserve the white of the paper for highlights. Paint the pumpkin stems with a brown mixture of alizarin crimson, cadmium orange, cadmium yellow and Prussian blue.

4 Add Browns

Paint the barrel with a mixture of all four colors and a large bamboo brush. Paint the grass area a more neutral orange-green color with a mixture of cadmium orange, cadmium yellow, Prussian blue and just a touch of alizarin crimson. Just suggest the grass, leaving lots of white space. Paint the apples with a no. 10 round and a mixture of all four colors, using mostly alizarin crimson.

5 Add Shading

Add shading to the pumpkins to imply depth with a mixture of alizarin crimson, cadmium orange and Prussian blue and a no. 6 or no. 10 round. Add shading to the apples with a mixture of all four colors, using predominantly alizarin crimson and a little more Prussian blue than you used to paint them in step 4.

6 Add Details to Barrel

Paint the line work on the barrel with a darker brown mixture of all four colors and no. 6 and no. 10 round brushes. Add details and shading to the grass with a dark green mixture of all four colors, using mostly Prussian blue. The blue will make the green color of the grass a bit deeper, creating cool shadows.

7 Add Finishing Touches

Add a darker wash over the barrel. Make the shadows on the pumpkins and apples darker with mixtures of alizarin crimson and Prussian blue. Define the shadows in the grass with a darker version of the green mixture from step 6. Erase the pencil lines and sign and date your painting.

Fall Pumpkins
11" x 14" (28cm x 36cm)
300-lb. (640gsm) cold-press watercolor paper

Painting a Landscape

It's rewarding to transform a sheet of white paper into a chilly winter scene with just a few applications of paint. Perhaps you live in an area that never sees snow. Or maybe you'll end up wanting to try this demonstration in the summertime. If so, you obviously won't be able to observe snow outside your window. When your real-life options are limited, look for reference materials in books, magazines, calendars and greeting cards to help you understand how light reflects off snow and what the shadows look like.

These reference materials will remind you that, for instance, shadows on snow usually have a blue tint, and this information will help make your painting accurate. To add to the mood and feel of the painting, heat up some hot chocolate and put on some warm slippers. Once you've finished this demonstration, try painting your own winter scenes.

Tips

Planning your white space for this painting will be even more important than for the last demonstration. You're going to use the white of your paper to represent the snow which is a large part of this scene. The only times I use cerulean blue and yellow ochre in this painting are for the shadows in the evergreen trees and for a few finishing touches. I recommend a limited palette because using every color you have whenever you feel like it will make your color composition noisy. Instead, plan your color scheme before you start painting, occasionally adding a splash or two of interesting colors, like the cerulean blue and yellow ochre in this painting.

Materials List

Paper
9" x 12" (23cm x 30cm) 140-lb. (300gsm)
    cold-press watercolor paper
Image Size for Matting and Framing
8" x 10" (20cm x 25cm)

Paints
brown madder
cadmium yellow
cerulean blue
Prussian blue
yellow ochre

Brushes
no. 2 round
no. 6 round
no. 10 round

Lessons & Techniques

Structural Drawing (page 21)
Drawing Linear Perspective (page 24)
Understanding Value (page 26)
Painting Atmospheric Perspective (page 29)
Understanding Color Temperature (page 32)
Painting Wet-on-Dry (page 48)
Applying a Variegated Wash (page 51)
Positive and Negative Painting (page 54)

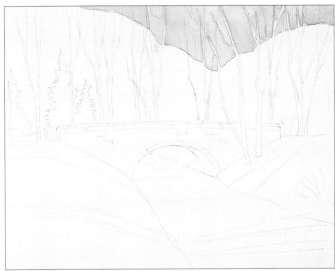

1 Draw Structure

Draw or transfer the image onto watercolor paper.

2 Paint Sky

Paint the sky with a no. 10 round and a light wash of Prussian blue. You'll paint the limbs later, but leave parts of them white now to indicate highlights and snow sitting on the branches.

3 Paint Background

Paint the background hills with a no. 10 round and a mixture of Prussian blue and brown madder. Remember to leave the trees white.

4 Add Interest

Paint the evergreen trees with a no. 10 round and a mixture of Prussian blue, cerulean blue, cadmium yellow and yellow ochre. I decided to add two more evergreen trees on the right to balance the painting.

5 Paint Tree Trunks

Paint some extra tree trunks in the distance with no. 2 and no. 6 round brushes and a mixture of Prussian blue and brown madder. Make a relatively cool mixture that favors blue more than brown. Atmospheric perspective tells you that distant elements should be bluish gray with a neutral value, and the closer elements should have more intense color and contrast.

6 Paint Bridge

Apply a variegated wash of yellow ochre, brown madder and a slight amount of Prussian blue over the bridge with a no. 10 round. The bridge's color is warm, so it will appear closer than the cooler background.

7 Add Details to Bridge

Add some character to the stones of the bridge with a no. 6 round and a mixture of Prussian blue and brown madder. You can indicate texture without actually painting every stone.

8 Paint Shadows

Paint shadows in the foreground with a no. 6 round and Prussian blue. Follow the contour lines of the snow as you paint.

9 Paint Trees

Fill in the trees that you left white earlier. Use no. 2 and no. 6 round brushes and a mixture of Prussian blue and brown madder to paint dark, broken lines, leaving light areas to imply sunlight and snow on the branches.

10 Add Accents

Add details to the bridge and paint the bushes with a no. 2 round and a mixture of brown madder and Prussian blue. Add shadows to the evergreens with a no. 6 round and a mixture of Prussian blue, cerulean blue, brown madder and yellow ochre.

11 Add Finishing Touches

Add whatever little touches you think will bring your painting together. I added light washes of yellow ochre on some parts of the background and over the bush in the foreground. When you're happy with the painting, erase extra pencil lines and sign and date your painting.

Snowy Stony Bridge
8" x 10" (20cm x 25cm)
140-lb. (300gsm) cold-press watercolor paper

Planning a Painting

What I really like about this painting's composition is the subtlety of the cat watching the bird in the tree. The viewer really has to look at the painting to get it, and then the viewer has the pleasure of an "ah ha!" moment. The viewer really feels like he or she is sharing something with the artist. Adding little surprises to your compositions will keep your viewers on their toes.

Have fun with the challenge of painting a slightly more complicated scene. Do this demonstration more than once and see how much progress you make next time.

Tips

Do thumbnail value and color sketches before you start on the actual painting to help you decide what will work best. Then use these materials for reference as you paint. The cat is the focal point of the composition, so I especially wanted it to look good. Before starting the actual painting, spend some time on a color sketch of the cat. You'll feel much more confident going into the painting. Some paint may spill onto the window frames as you paint. To fix this you can press firmly on the area with a rag to pull up the wet paint. If the paint is still noticeable, scrape the paper with a craft knife after it dries. Scraping to correct paint spills works here because the frames will remain white. Be careful when scraping an area over which you'll apply more paint later. The area will be rough and the paint may not lay right. Don't base your success on a comparison between your results and my painting. You can look at my example for pointers and tips, but your painting doesn't have to look like mine to be interesting and successful.

Materials List

Paper
9" x 12" (23cm x 30cm) 140-lb. (300gsm) cold-press watercolor paper
Image Size for Matting and Framing
10" x 8" (25cm x 20cm)

Paints
alizarin crimson
brown madder
burnt sienna
cadmium orange
cadmium yellow
Prussian blue
yellow ochre

Brushes
no. 2 round
no. 6 round
no. 10 round
large bamboo brush

Other
craft knife
rag
salt
scraps of watercolor paper
sketch paper
straight edge

Lessons & Techniques

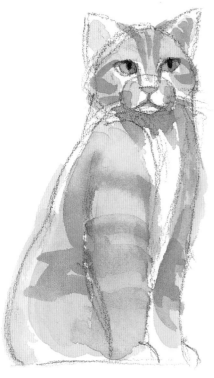

1 Gather References

Planning ahead will help answer questions that could arise while you're painting. I gather reference material from books, magazines and photographs. In this case, I looked for references of cats, birds, windows, trees and shrubs. It's extremely helpful to sketch the subject or other elements before putting them into your painting.

2 Do Preliminary Sketches

Draw small, quick thumbnail value sketches on sketch paper to work out values and your composition. I decided to use the third sketch. I like the size and arrangement of elements.

3 Draw Color Sketches

I redrew the thumbnail sketch from page 111 as a structural drawing without indicating values. Then I applied a few different color schemes, following the value pattern I had established. I like the second sketch best, though the color composition of the third is also pleasing.

4 Paint Window Panes

Paint the window panes around the cat and window frames with a no. 10 round and Prussian blue. Make the value gradate as you move up the window. The easiest way is to lay multiple washes as you move up until each window pane is the value you want. Remember to let each wash dry completely before laying down the next one.

5 Paint Bricks
Lay a variegated wash of brown madder, burnt sienna, Prussian blue and yellow ochre over the bricks with a large bamboo brush. While the paint is still wet, add salt for texture. Wipe off the remaining salt after the painting has dried.

6 Add Accents
Lay second washes over individual bricks with a no. 6 round brush, taking colors from different parts of the variegated mixture from step 5 for different bricks. You don't have to paint every brick. Let some of the original wash show to provide variety. Remember to paint around the mortar between the bricks.

7 Paint Shutter
Apply a mixture of brown madder and burnt sienna over the shutter with a no. 10 round. If you want, leave some white space to indicate highlights. Make sure you paint straight lines. Paint the shutter in portions so it will seem less intimidating. A straight edge will help you paint straight lines.

8 Paint Cat

Add shadows to the shutter with no. 2 and no. 6 rounds and a mixture of brown madder and Prussian blue. Remember that the light source is shining from the upper left. Paint the cat with a wash of yellow ochre, cadmium orange and brown madder and no. 6 and no. 10 rounds. Make sure to leave the window frames white. Apply a darker value of this mixture wet-on-wet to paint the cat's stripes.

9 Darken Stripes

Let the previous step dry. Make the cat's stripes more noticeable by applying washes of clear water followed by washes of burnt sienna, using a no. 10 round. This wet-on-wet technique will soften the edges of the stripes so they look more like fur.

10 Add Details

Paint the cat's eyes with a mixture of yellow ochre, cadmium yellow and burnt sienna and a no. 2 round. Leave a small amount of white space to indicate highlights on the eyes. Paint the nose and mouth with a mixture of alizarin crimson and yellow ochre and a no. 2 round. Use the same mixture to paint the ears with a no. 6 round. Add shadows and define the facial features with the same colors and no. 2 and no. 6 rounds.

11 Add Silhouette

Paint the silhouette reflection on the window with a no. 6 round brush and a mixture of Prussian blue and brown madder. Start with the bird to make sure you get the proportion and placement right. Add shadows to the window frames and sill. Don't forget the shadows on the cat from the window frames. Erase extra pencil lines and sign and date another successful painting.

Window Shopping
10" x 8" (25cm x 20cm)
140-lb. (300gsm) cold-press watercolor paper

Painting a Still Life

The shapes of these objects will provide a good challenge to sharpen your drawing skills and to observe how the surfaces interact with each other, with the light source and with the shadows. You might want to find some shiny metal and glass objects to set up your own still life. Study how these objects reflect the light. The metal surface reflects the objects around it while distorting their shapes. Notice how the colors of objects behind glass come through. In the structural drawing I indicated which areas to leave untouched by paint. This kind of planning will help you paint the shine on the glass so it indicates the outline of the bottle. The matte finish of the books doesn't react with surrounding objects the same way as shiny objects, but this contrast makes the painting more interesting. I chose to paint the background with a dark color to contrast the light urn and the reflections from the glass.

Materials List

Paper
10" x 14" (25cm x 36cm) 140-lb. (300gsm) cold-press watercolor paper
Image Size for Matting and Framing
8" x 10" (20cm x 25cm)

Paints
brown madder
burnt sienna
cadmium orange
cadmium yellow
Prussian blue
yellow ochre

Brushes
no. 6 round
no. 10 round
large bamboo brush

Tips

Avoid tangents, like placing the candlestick at the side of the urn so their edges share a line. Centering the candlestick on the urn also would have looked unnatural. Instead, I placed the candlestick about a third of the way down from the edge of the urn to make a pleasing composition. For your structural drawing, draw the highlights the same as you would draw any other object or element. This will help you preserve the white of the paper for these areas. To enhance depth, use warm, aggressive colors in the foreground and cool, recessive colors in the background.

Lessons & Techniques

Structural Drawing (page 21)
Drawing Linear Perspective (page 24)
Understanding Value (page 26)
Painting Atmospheric Perspective (page 29)
Understanding Color Temperature (page 32)
Planning Composition (page 34)

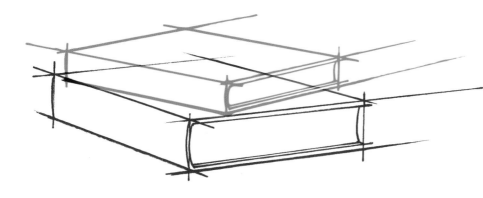

Observe Each Object Separately
Think of the books as two simple boxes, each box with its own perspective.

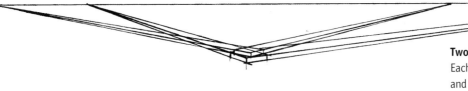

Two Two-Point Perspectives
Each book is drawn in two-point perspective, and each has its own vanishing points to make a total of four. All four still fall on the horizon.

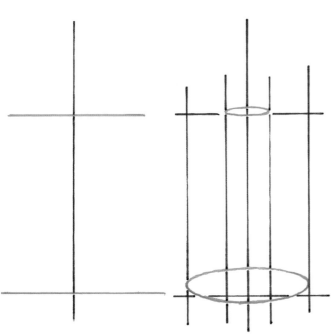

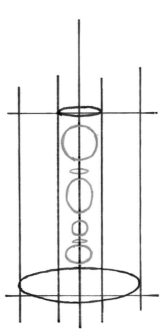

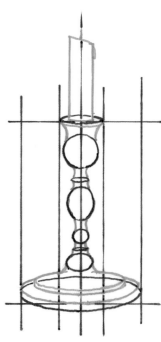

Draw Symmetrical Objects
This method for drawing a symmetrical candlestick works for all symmetrical objects. Draw a vertical line to serve as the center of your subject. Draw two horizontal lines to serve as the top and bottom of your subject.

Draw Widths
Draw two more vertical lines equidistant from the center line to denote the width of the base of the candlestick. Draw another pair of vertical lines to show the width of the top of the candlestick. Draw ellipses for the base and top of the candlestick.

Add Form
Draw circles and ovals around the center line to add form.

Finish Contour
Join the circles and ovals and add the candle to finish the drawing.

1 Paint Urn

Transfer the line drawing onto watercolor paper. Paint the urn on the right with a mixture of yellow ochre, burnt sienna, brown madder and Prussian blue and a no. 10 round. As you draw the highlights and paint around them, remember that the light source is shining from the upper left.

2 Paint Candlestick and Background

Paint the candlestick with a mixture of yellow ochre, cadmium yellow and cadmium orange and a no. 6 round. Add a small amount of burnt sienna to the mixture to paint the dark areas. Preserve highlight areas on the candlestick. I also left a thin white line between the candlestick and the urn to help define the candlestick's shape. Once the candlestick has dried, paint the candle with a mixture of Prussian blue and yellow ochre and a no. 6 round. I also left a thin line of white around the candle.

Paint in the background using a variegated mixture of Prussian blue, brown madder and burnt sienna. Use a large bamboo brush for the big areas and a no. 10 round for the smaller areas.

3 Paint Books

Paint the sides of the books with a no. 10 round. Paint the bottom book with a mixture of brown madder, burnt sienna and Prussian blue. Paint the top book with a mixture of yellow ochre, brown madder, burnt sienna and Prussian blue. Because the light source is coming from the upper left, the right sides of the books are in shadow, so the mixtures for these sides should be darker and cooler, with more Prussian blue. When these areas have dried, paint the covers of the books with darker versions of the same mixtures and a no. 6 round.

4 Paint Glass
Paint the background behind the bottle with a no. 10 round. Look for the highlights as you paint. Paint the book underneath the bottle and the cork the same color as the rest of the book with a no. 6 round. Also use this color to add the books' shadow on the urn. Leave a line of white around the edges of the bottle to help define its form.

5 Add Additional Washes
To add more detail and form, add darker washes of the original mixtures to parts of each element. Accent the urn with a no. 10 round, using a no. 6 round for the dark lines. Accent the candle, candlestick and the wick with a no. 6 round. Add accents to the books with no. 6 and no. 10 rounds. Paint details and add more washes to the bottle with a no. 6 round. Darker washes on the bottle will help the highlights stand out and make it look more like glass.

6 Add Washes to Background
Paint more washes over the background with a large bamboo brush and a no. 10 round. Darken the areas around the subject matter to create contrast.

7 Add Finishing Touches
Add the shadows of the books, glass and candlestick and add details like the dark lines underneath the urn and books to better define their shapes. Add any other washes you think you need. I needed to darken the part of the background that you can see through the bottle. Sign and date your painting and take a step back to admire it!

Relics
8" x 10" (20cm x 25cm)
140-lb. (300gsm) cold-press watercolor paper

Painting a Still Life With Vegetables

The makings of a great salad are also the makings of a great still life. These subjects are easily available and fun to draw. Try getting your own vegetables and fruits and setting them up exactly as I have on page 121, putting the light source on the right. Drawing and painting from your own three-dimensional still life will teach you so much more than painting from a two-dimensional picture in a book. This demonstration also will give you insight into the difference between painting dull surfaces and painting glossy surfaces. Bon Appetit!

Tips

Again avoid tangents and make sure you draw the highlight areas in your structural drawing. I highly recommend setting up your own still life and painting from it, using the steps in this demonstration as a guide as you paint your own. The point of a still life is to observe what's in front of you, really taking the time to see what's going on with light, color and composition. Painting from your own still life will provide you with this experience much more than painting from this book can. You'll paint each vegetable with layers of washes to get the desired impact and value, so don't worry if it looks too washed out at first.

Materials List

Paper
10" x 14" (25cm x 36cm) 140-lb. (300gsm)
  cold-press watercolor paper
Image Size for Matting and Framing
8" x 10" (20cm x 25cm)

Paints
alizarin crimson
burnt sienna
cadmium orange
cadmium red
cadmium yellow
hooker's green
Prussian blue

Brushes
no. 6 round
no. 10 round

Other
cabbage
carrots
cauliflower
eggplant
orange pepper
red pepper
yellow pepper

Lessons & Techniques

Structural Drawing (page 21)
Understanding Color (page 30)
Planning Composition (page 34)

Draw in Stages

Sketch all of the basic shapes first (left) and then sketch in the details (right). Drawing in the details will include reworking a lot of the lines of the basic shapes, but starting with the basic shapes ensures a sound overall composition and accurate proportions and shapes for the vegetables.

1 Draw Structure

Draw or transfer the image onto watercolor paper.

2 Paint Yellow Pepper

Paint the yellow pepper with a predominantly yellow mixture of cadmium yellow, cadmium red and cadmium orange and a no. 10 round. Paint around the highlight areas, which are essential to communicate the glossy surface of the pepper.

3 Paint Reds and Oranges

Paint the red pepper with a mixture of alizarin crimson, cadmium red and cadmium orange. Leave just a hairline of white between the yellow and red peppers. If the paint of both is still wet, the colors will bleed into each other a bit. This effect only occurs in watercolors, and it's one of the qualities that makes the medium so popular and fun to work with. When the painting is finished, the bleed will look like a red reflection on the yellow pepper.

Paint the orange pepper and carrots with a mixture of cadmium red and cadmium orange and a no. 10 round. Paint both with the same mixture, simply watering down the mixture to make a lighter value for the carrots.

4 Paint Remaining Vegetables

Paint the cauliflower with a mixture of cadmium yellow and slight amounts of hooker's green and burnt sienna and a no. 10 round. Follow its contours with your brushstrokes, leaving highlight areas untouched. Paint the cabbage with a mixture of hooker's green, cadmium yellow and a slight amount of alizarin crimson. The surface of cabbage isn't glossy, so I didn't leave any highlights. The cauliflower was still wet when I painted the cabbage, so I let the green bleed into the cauliflower. The color will make a good shadow on the cauliflower. When the cabbage and cauliflower dry, paint the eggplant with a deep purple mixture of alizarin crimson, Prussian blue and a slight amount of hooker's green.

5 Add Greens

When the paint from step 4 dries, use no. 6 and no. 10 round brushes to paint washes of green over the stems and greenery with a mixture of hooker's green, cadmium yellow and a slight amount of alizarin crimson. While you're working with this green mixture, add some washes to the cabbage.

6 Add More Color

Paint additional washes on the carrots and orange and yellow peppers with a mixture of alizarin crimson, cadmium red, cadmium orange, cadmium yellow and some Prussian blue to darken it. Paint the darkest parts of the red pepper with a mixture of alizarin crimson and Prussian blue. When the cabbage and yellow pepper dry, paint the shadow on the cauliflower with a no. 10 round and a mixture of hooker's green, Prussian blue and alizarin crimson.

7 Shade Greens

Add more washes of green over the cabbage and the greenery on the other vegetables with a no. 10 round and a mixture of hooker's green, Prussian blue, alizarin crimson and cadmium yellow.

8 Add Shading

Add shadows on and under each vegetable, especially on the green areas with a mixture of Prussian blue, alizarin crimson and hooker's green. Add some shading on the eggplant with the same mixture. Use a lighter value of this mixture to define the cabbage's shadow on the cauliflower. At this point I considered adding color to the background to define the shape of the cauliflower. Instead, I added a small leaf on its lower right to frame it. This detail and the similar color of the shadows and the eggplant really help bring the composition together. Sign and date your last painting.

Fresh Produce
8" x 10" (20cm x 25cm)
140-lb. (300gsm) cold-press watercolor paper

Glossary

Aggressive Colors warm colors that appear to come forward visually

Analogous Colors a range of colors adjacent to each other on the color wheel: blue-green, blue, blue-violet and violet, for example

Atmospheric Perspective depth implied through value and color temperature

Back Run an instance in which paint at the edge of a freshly applied wash runs back into the wash area, which has begun to dry, creating a watermark; you can avoid back runs by pulling up any extra paint and water with a dry brush before it flows back into the wash

Bamboo Brush a paintbrush with a round handle made from bamboo; when wet, the coarse hairs should taper to a point

Block a pad of watercolor paper in which the sheets are glued together on all four sides so the paper will wrinkle less when made wet; you can remove the top sheet after the painting has dried by inserting a knife between the top two sheets and running it around the four sides

Cake a hard, dry version of watercolor pigment

Chroma color or color intensity

Cold-Press Watercolor Paper paper that has a moderately rough surface texture

Color Mixing mixing one or more paint colors with water to achieve the desired transparency, color and value

Color Scheme a family of colors used together in a painting, also referred to as a painting's palette

Color Sketch a small, quick, preliminary painting used to plan the colors of a composition

Color Theory principles of how colors relate to one another

Color Wheel a circular chart showing the primary, secondary and tertiary colors and how they relate to one another

Complementary Colors two colors that appear opposite each other on the color wheel, red and green, for example

Composition an arrangement of elements, including structure, value and color, that provides a path for the eye to follow through the painting

Contrast the existence of extreme differences between specific elements of a painting, most commonly used to discuss value

Cool Colors colors that look cool, such as green, blue and violet, also referred to as recessive colors

Crop expose or display only part of a painting, photograph or scene

Drybrush a term to describe an application of paint to a dry surface using a brush loaded with paint and very little water

Ellipse a circle placed at an angle to show perspective

Flat Brush a paintbrush with bristles that form a wide, flat edge, as opposed to a round brush with bristles that form a point

Flat Wash a wash of paint and water that is even in value and color

Focal Point the area or part of a painting to which the composition leads the eye, also referred to as the center of interest

Foreshorten to give the appearance of depth and projection by shortening the visible area of an element; imagine a door and doorway. When the door is closed, the door is the same width as the doorway. As you open the door, the apparent width of the door becomes less wide compared to the door frame

Gradate to create a transition from one value or color to another

Gradated Wash a wash that changes value

Grade the quality of materials, such as professional grade or student grade

Hake Brush (pronounced hockey) a wide, flat paintbrush with coarse hairs and a paddle-shaped, wooden handle

Hard Edge the sharply defined edge of a wash or stroke of paint that dried without its edges being blended

Highlight an area of reflected light on an object

Horizon Line the line where land or water meet the sky, in reference to linear perspective

Hot-Press Watercolor Paper paper that has a smooth surface texture

Imprint to create texture by pressing an item, such as a sponge, loaded with paint against a painting surface

Intensity the potency or strength of a color

Kneaded Eraser a soft, pliable gray eraser that damages watercolor paper less than other erasers because it's less abrasive and doesn't crumble

Lead the graphite in a pencil and also the scale that rates the hardness or softness of the graphite: 6B, 5B, 4B, 3B, 2B, B, HB, H, 2H, 3H, 4H, 5H and 6H from soft to hard

Leading Lines a group of compositional elements used to form lines to direct the viewer's eye to points of interest

Lightfastness the degree to which a paint resists fading

Light Source the origin of the light shining on elements in a composition

Linear Perspective depth implied through line and the relative size of elements in a painting

Measure to determine specific proportions of elements in a scene

Mixture a combination of watercolor paint and water

Mop Quil Brush a round paintbrush with soft hairs that form a point when wet, known for holding lots of fluid

Monochromatic painting a painting done with different values of one color

Natural Hair Brush a paintbrush made of natural animal hairs

Negative Painting painting around shapes or elements to imply their forms

Neutral Colors browns and grays made from combinations of the three primary colors

One-Point Perspective a type of linear perspective with one vanishing point

Pad a stack of sheets of watercolor paper attached at one side with glue or wire

Paper Weight the thickness of a sheet of paper; common weights are the thin 90-lb. (190gsm), the moderate 140-lb. (300gsm) and the thick 300-lb. (640gsm)

Plein Air a french term meaning "open air," used to describe painting on site

Positive Painting painting an element against a lighter background, as opposed to negative painting

Primary Colors the three basic colors—red, yellow and blue—from which all other colors are derived

Recessive Colors cool colors that appear to recede visually

Reflected Light light reflected off one element onto another

Rough Watercolor Paper paper that has a rough surface texture

Round Brush a paintbrush that has fine, stiff bristles that come to a point, as opposed to a flat brush with bristles that form an edge

Scrub to move a brush back and forth over a wash to remove some of the paint; this technique can damage both the brush and the paper's surface

Secondary Colors the three colors made from a combination of two primary colors: orange, green and violet

Soft Edge the edge of a wash that has been smoothly blended into the surrounding area

Solubility the degree to which paint dissolves and mixes with water

Spatter to create texture by applying random dots of paint

Stencil to create texture by covering parts of the surface with a patterned material, such as an onion bag, and applying paint over it

Stretch to attach wet paper to a board so it won't wrinkle as it dries

Structural Drawing a drawing of the shapes and forms in a scene without value or color

Synthetic Hair Brush a paintbrush made with artificial bristles

Tangent the point at which two compositional elements touch or intersect; tangents usually detract from a composition.

Tertiary Colors the colors made from combinations of one primary color and one secondary color: blue-violet, for example

Thumbnail Sketch a small, quick sketch used to plan a composition

Transfer Sheet a sheet of tracing paper covered with graphite on one side, used to transfer an image onto your painting surface

Tube a container of soft, moist watercolor paint

Two-Point Perspective a type of linear perspective with two vanishing points

Value the lightness or darkness of a color

Value Scale a scale showing the range of values of a color

Value Sketch a pencil sketch used to plan the lights and darks of a painting

Vanishing Point a point on the horizon line at which parallel lines seem to converge

Variegated Wash a wash that changes color

Viewfinder a device used to crop a scene

Warm Colors colors that look warm, such as red, orange, and yellow, also referred to as aggressive colors

Wash an application of a paint and water mixture

Wet-on-Dry a term to describe an application of paint to a dry surface using a brush loaded with paint and a normal amount of water

Wet-on-Wet a term to describe an application of paint to a wet surface using a brush loaded with paint and a normal amount of water

Index

Beginner's Guide to Drawing & Painting. Copyright © 2009 by North Light Books. Manufactured in China. All rights reserved. No part of this book may be reproduced in any form or by any electronic or mechanical means including information storage and retrieval systems without permission in writing from the publisher, except by a reviewer who may quote brief passages in a review. Published by North Light Books, an imprint of F+W Media, Inc., 4700 East Galbraith Road, Cincinnati, Ohio, 45236. (800) 289-0963. First Edition.

Other fine North Light Books are available from your favorite bookstore, art supply store or online supplier.

14   13   12   11   10   5   4   3   2   1

All works of art reproduced in this book have been previously copyrighted by Mark and Mary Willenbrink.

DISTRIBUTED IN CANADA BY FRASER DIRECT
100 Armstrong Avenue
Georgetown, ON, Canada L7G 5S4
Tel: (905) 877-4411

fw

media DISTRIBUTED IN THE U.K. AND EUROPE BY DAVID & CHARLES
Brunel House, Newton Abbot, Devon, TQ12 4PU, England
Tel: (+44) 1626 323200, Fax: (+44) 1626 323319
Email: postmaster@davidandcharles.co.uk

DISTRIBUTED IN AUSTRALIA BY CAPRICORN LINK
P.O. Box 704, S. Windsor NSW, 2756 Australia
Tel: (02) 4577-3555

Library of Congress Cataloging-in-Publication Data

Willenbrink, Mark and Mary
    Drawing for the Absolute Beginner / Mark and Mary Willenbrink.— 1st ed.
        p. cm
    Includes index.
    ISBN-13: 978-1-58180-789-9 (pb. : alk. paper)
    ISBN-10: 1-58180-789-9 (pb. : alk. paper)
    1. Drawing—Technique. I. Title.

ND2237 .B67 2001
571.42'24328—dc21   00-068694

Willenbrink, Mark.
    Watercolor for the absolute beginner / Mark Willenbrink written with Mary Willenbrink.—1st ed.
        p. cm.
    Includes index.
    ISBN 1-58180-341-9 (pbk. : alk. paper)
    1. Watercolor painting—Technique. I. Willenbrink, Mary. II. Title.

ND2420 .W548 2003
751.42'2—dc21   2003048796